National Preservation Office

digital culture: maximising the nation's investment

a synthesis of JISC/NPO studies on the preservation of electronic materials

edited by Mary Feeney

Acknowledgement

The studies summarised here are funded by the Joint Information Services Committee of the Higher Education Funding Councils and administered by the British Library Research and Innovation Centre.

First published 1999 by
The National Preservation Office
The British Library
96 Euston Road
London NW1 2DB

ISBN 0-7123-4645-7

contents

Foreword p4

1. Introduction to the issues p8
2. Stakeholders: rights and responsibilities p18
3. Encouraging and learning from best practice p31
4. Technological decisions p41
5. Estimating the costs of digital preservation p50
6. Rescuing digital materials p61
7. Completing the jigsaw: managing the digital preservation process p72
8. Key recommendations and follow-up activities p78

Appendices

1. Studies on the preservation of electronic materials commissioned by the Digital Archiving Working Group p81
2. References and bibliography p82
3. Acronyms p84
4. Members of the Digital Archiving Working Group p86

foreword

In the last years of this millennium, we are either at the beginning of – or in the middle of, depending on whom you listen to – a digital revolution. In future, we are told, we shall acquire all our information and entertainment in digital form from a screen. Throughout the developed world projects are under way to create 'virtual libraries', containing digital representations of museum objects, works of art, texts and moving images. Such developments are undoubtedly bringing to a far wider audience items and texts that are currently accessible to a relative few. Initiatives such as those set out in the Library and Information Commission's report *New library: the people's network* (1997) and new sources of finance through, for example, the New Opportunities Fund of the National Lottery represent enormously important developments in widening access to such materials.

The initiatives continue and build upon the massive investment made in recent years by public and private sector organisations in the creation and acquisition of digital resources, to the extent that such resources now form a significant and growing part of our cultural and intellectual heritage. The opportunities presented by digital technology have also come to be seen by some as a panacea, as not just a means of providing access to materials that they believe have lain unused and unusable in libraries, archives and museums all over the world, but also as a means of preserving them forever. However, there is already evidence that electronic information created or acquired with public money is being lost through neglect or through a lack of awareness of the need to take active steps to ensure its preservation.

Traditional library and archive materials (paper, vellum, even papyrus) and the materials used to bind them together (cloth and leather) present many preservation problems, with which conservators and preservation administrators have been wrestling for years, but as far as paper-based information resources are concerned the solutions are generally well understood. As we move towards ever greater dependence on electronic sources of information, however, we encounter preservation problems of a completely different order of magnitude and a completely different type. The problems of brittle paper and decaying bindings are serious ones, but, nevertheless, the timescale for most papers becoming brittle or their bindings degrading, if they are stored in reasonable conditions, is at least a good number of decades, if not several centuries. With electronic information the timescale is very much shorter.

The main problem is that of obsolescence. Systems change rapidly and there is no guarantee that today's software will be readable by tomorrow's hardware.

There has been concern about digital preservation in the library community for some years, but a serious and active interest is a relatively recent phenomenon. In 1996 the Commission on Preservation and Access (CPA) and the Research Libraries Group (RLG) in the USA published a joint report on *Preserving digital information* which identified problems, made recommendations and suggested areas for further research (Waters and Garrett, 1996). In the UK, in November 1995, the JISC (Joint Information Services Committee) of the Higher Education Funding Councils and the British Library addressed the question of the preservation of digital media by holding a national conference in Warwick, where a number of action points were identified (Fresko, 1996).

The first of these was an analysis of the CPA/RLG report (then nearing completion) to identify those recommendations in it which were relevant to the UK situation and where research could usefully be undertaken to complement, but not duplicate, that in progress or planned elsewhere, particularly in the USA and Australia (Matthews *et al.*, 1997). A part of this analysis resulted in the holding of a seminar in December 1996 at the British Library, which was attended by representatives from the library and archive profession, data archives, and publishers, and where it was agreed that the JISC would fund a number of studies on digital archiving, in collaboration with the National Preservation Office (NPO), and the library, archival and publishing communities.

Those studies form the basis of this book. A full list is given on page 80. The programme of 'JISC/NPO Studies on the Preservation of Electronic Materials' was guided by a specially established committee, the Digital Archiving Working Group, which contained experts in the field from higher education, data archives, the Public Record Office, the National Preservation Office, the British Library and the Publishers' Association (for a list of members see page 85). It reported to the Management Committee of the National Preservation Office. The programme was administered by the British Library Research and Innovation Centre and funded by JISC through the Electronic Libraries (eLib) Programme.

The first study (Bennett, 1997) developed a framework of data types and formats, in order to indicate the likely problems, requirements and responsibilities appropriate to each category, and to identify the most appropriate method of preservation. Closely related to this was a comparison of preservation methods and costing models (Hendley, 1998), which aimed, on the basis of a matrix of data types, to draw up a decision model to assess the most appropriate method of long term preservation and to produce a further model for comparing the costs of the preferred methods of preservation.

Two studies were concerned with the needs of data creators and the responsibility for archiving of such data. In the traditional area of publishing it is quite clear where the responsibility for maintaining an archive of published information lies: publishers do not regard it as residing with them, and if libraries wish to preserve the books or journals they have bought, then it is their responsibility to do so. In electronic publishing the issues are not nearly as clear. In many cases, for example, libraries do not hold the database – that resides with the publisher. What happens if the publisher goes out of business or loses interest in maintaining the database because the income stream from it has dried up? The report emanating from this study (Haynes *et al.*, 1997) recommended that a national body be established in the UK to coordinate such archiving and that it should be funded from the public sector, with an extension of legal deposit legislation to cover electronic publications. As far as unpublished data are concerned, universities and the funding agencies which support scholarly research are major sponsors of digital resource creation and, therefore, have a responsibility for ensuring that the research they help to create is preserved on a long-term basis. The Data Archive at the University of Essex (1998) sought to establish how much of these digital resources were being created, as well as the level of provision which is being made for their preservation. The report also considered what the future needs of these bodies were with regard to digital preservation.

A further study (Beagrie and Greenstein, 1998) produced a strategic policy framework, which examined how different organisations are approaching the key stages in the life-cycle of digital resources, from creation, through access to preservation. Finally, the question of post-hoc rescue or 'digital archaeology' was addressed (Ross and Gow, 1998). We are already in a situation where some data appears to be inaccessible due to the obsolescence of the hardware or software required to read them. The study examined approaches to accessing digital materials where the media have become damaged, through disaster or age, or where the hardware or software is either no longer available or unknown. It illustrated some methods of recovery, showing that most data can be rescued, if there is enough time and money, but emphasising that the value of the data must be weighed against the cost of recovery.

These were all fairly short-term studies, but, given the relative paucity of research in this area, it was considered essential for this basic work to be undertaken before any commitment to funding for practical experiments was made available. The studies are also quite technical, and so it was decided to compress the results of this research into this short book which, it is hoped, will be read by policy makers and funders both inside and outside the public sector.

These preliminary studies have prepared the ground for more extensive work at a practical level to assess the problems involved in the long-term preservation of electronic information. That work is now being undertaken in several parts of the world. In the UK, JISC is funding the CEDARS project (CURL Exemplars in Digital ARchiveS), which will produce both recommendations and guidelines as well as practical and scaleable models for establishing digital archives.

A clear message that emerged from the studies was that a great deal of money can be wasted if digitisation projects are undertaken without due regard to the long-term preservation of the digital files. It is relatively easy to produce a digital version of a book, manuscript or museum object. Unfortunately it is also easy to do so in such a way that either the long-term preservation of the file becomes expensive, because of the way it was created, or with the result that the work will have to be repeated because no plan was in place for archiving the file.

But digital preservation is about much more than digitising to facilitate the preservation of items which were originally produced in a different medium. The preservation of digital materials which were created in the digital domain provides an even greater challenge, since there is no opportunity to return to the non-digital original. As our world moves increasingly towards dealing with this 'born-digital' information, the potentially devastating impact on the future of scholarship increases, and so must our sense of duty to solve these problems.

It is the hope of the Digital Archiving Working Group, which commissioned this book, that it will cause those who are about to embark on a digitisation project to consider the long-term archiving of the files they are about to create. The Group also hopes that it will encourage bodies that are about to fund digitisation programmes to ensure that all proposals include a workable archiving strategy.

Peter Fox *Chairman*
Digital Archiving Working Group *February 1999*

1 introduction to the issues

1.1 Digital preservation – a contradiction in terms?

Digital information forms an increasingly large part of our cultural and intellectual heritage and offers significant benefits to users. The use of computers is changing forever the way information is created, managed and accessed. The ability to generate, amend and copy information in digital form, to search texts and databases, and to transmit information rapidly over networks has led to a dramatic growth in the application of digital technologies.

At the same time, the experience of addressing the 'millennium bug' in existing software systems, or of losing data through poor management, is beginning to raise awareness of the fragility of this medium, compared to traditional media such as paper. Electronic information is fragile and evanescent. It needs a proactive and strategic approach from its inception to secure its preservation over the longer term.

Although experience in creating and managing specific forms of digital data has been built up over a number of decades in the sciences and social sciences, in many areas it is a relatively new medium where much of the future life-cycle, activities and cost models are currently unknown. These factors have led to increasing concern about the potential loss of our 'collective memory' in the Digital Age.

The situation is encapsulated in a draft policy statement by the Australian National Preservation Office (1997):

'As the twentieth century draws to a close, an ever-increasing quantity of information is created, stored, disseminated and networked in digital form. Digital objects, many of which are dynamic in nature, are created by a variety of creators for a number of purposes. Digital objects include data stored in digital form and accessed using electronic equipment. Examples are databases, images, sound, video, documents, etc....

The organisations charged with the responsibility of preserving and making available [our] cultural and intellectual heritage will need to develop a range of strategies to address the preservation of and access to various categories of digital objects. Custodial and non-custodial arrangements will need to be considered both from a preservation and an access perspective and will need to be considered prior to creation if possible and throughout the life of the object.'

The digital world is one of sustained change and flux. Technology is constantly changing; the legal environment is subject to revision and change; digital objects are themselves dynamic. In this context 'preservation' and 'digital materials' seem almost mutually exclusive – how can you preserve something that is constantly changing? And yet digitisation is itself a method of preservation, a way of providing alternative access to the original object. It can be used to preserve and make accessible information not originally produced in this way, especially in the case of originals at risk, such as those printed on acid paper.

The short term benefits of digital objects – manipulation, distribution, duplication, linking – are immense, but the long-term viability of such objects is fraught with difficulty because of the ever-changing technology needed for their storage and use. This apparent contradiction has prompted the search for strategies and processes that will help make digital preservation a reality.

This introductory chapter poses a number of basic questions in order to help provide an overall context for the discussion of preservation issues in connection with digital material. Later chapters examine the issues in more detail and recommend further actions and research.

1.2 Why preserve digital information?

Digital information can be generated by a number of different processes and for different reasons. The information may, for example, exist in a definitive version and be generated by a project or business function with a finite timespan; or it may be dynamic, constantly evolving, generated by a project or business function with no finite timescale. The purpose for which it is created and the reasons why it is preserved may also vary. Non-digital collections may be digitised to improve access or to preserve the information they contain; or collections may be made of existing digital information for future re-use and research.

Whatever the context, preservation is a response to the threat of destruction and loss. Recognising the threat elicits a response, the scale of which is usually in proportion to the value that is placed on the object under threat. Such actions incur costs, which will continue while the threat appears to remain. Funds will be drawn upon, and resources mobilised. Each part of the process will draw different stakeholders into the preservation activity.

With printed, paper-based material there is usually time to consider the best course of action and to make appropriate decisions. The threats to digital information are varied and subtle, and have much shorter timescales than for information on paper. This means that the costs of digital preservation come much earlier and more often, and that substantial costs may be incurred before the value of the object can be realised. Decisions are required, supported by expenditure, to enable resources to be deployed quickly in order to counter the threat of irreversible loss. The resources may involve substantial capital investment as well as specialist labour, both available in the near term only at a premium.

The contest for limited resources and the balancing of conflicting priorities introduce the question of selection: which material should be preserved? The solution is not straightforward for any collection developer, though with digital material the threat of loss is ever present and the volume of material requiring attention is growing year by year.

From this other questions grow, concerning the long term viability of any stored information, and the costs and benefits of long-term accessibility:

- What is the rationale for preservation?
- When an object is retrieved from the archive fifty or more years hence, will it still be valuable? Will it still be recognisable, comprehensible and usable?
- Different organisations, for example legal deposit libraries and other research libraries, have their own requirements when retaining material over long periods of time. In each case, what costs are involved? How do these costs apply to an item's life-cycle? How can they share the responsibility?
- Are the benefits measurable? How can they be achieved, and who is responsible for monitoring them?

1.3 Why is digital archiving different from preserving a book?

Books are examples of technological artefacts holding information whose design has matured slowly over hundreds of years. In general, no assisting technology is needed to access the information in a book. Preserving the artefact (simply storing it in good condition) preserves the information (excepting some cases such as loss of the actual language involved).

Digital technology, by contrast, has only been with us for tens rather than hundreds of years. The technological basis for computing is changing rapidly, advancing far faster than any previous technological developments. Information encoded in digital form – as information objects – is entirely dependent on technology to allow access. There are many ways in which continued access can be threatened: through damage to the medium on which it rests; through loss of the information which describes how to access it; or through loss of the computing environment – hardware and software – on which access depends.

Unlike the situation that applies to books, digital archiving requires relatively frequent investments to overcome rapid obsolescence introduced by galloping technological change.

1.4 What should be archived?

It is obvious to most that the digital equivalents of paper publications – books and journals especially – should be treated with the same respect and accorded the same preservation priorities as the paper versions. It is the information content we value, more than the medium or the format, and we must take adequate steps to preserve the newly emerging digital forms of our cultural heritage.

However, our responsibilities do not stop at digital versions of the books and journals currently preserved in their paper form via legal deposit and other mechanisms. There are many other kinds of information that are not currently covered by legislation or by Public Record Office guidelines. Examples include medical records that need to be preserved over time to study disease demographics, and data generated in the course of research. How should these be preserved? The materials preserved must include contextual information by which they can be understood and used correctly. This is vital, for example, where research data are preserved and used for secondary analysis or to replicate experiments. The Data Archive at the University of Essex is the longest established digital archive in the UK and has long experience of preserving and disseminating such research data.

Research projects in particular produce a huge amount of 'electronic paperwork', for example administrative files, electronic research diaries, automatic output from laboratory research instruments, electronic mail. Should these be preserved?

As these few examples illustrate, the volume of digital objects is such that universal preservation would be impossible – some kind of selection is inevitable. However, there are no common selection procedures or agreed guidelines on criteria for selection.

Selection requires qualitative assessment of the value of information. How should this be carried out? The creator of the information can play a key role in assessing its true value, and the research community certainly feels that it should be involved in any selection process regarding research data, but any decision is inevitably subjective. There are risks of censorship, or misjudgement on the part of individuals or organisations. At the same time it is often difficult, if not impossible, to predict the future usefulness of material. Would random selection be a better approach, at least for some types of digital information? One suggestion is for a sampling exercise: a national audit of digital materials, carried out at times specified by a national coordinating body to select those that should be archived according to agreed selection criteria which are evaluated and monitored continuously by the coordinating body.

There is certainly a high management cost associated with a selective policy. However, it is likely that the heavy operational costs of digital preservation techniques will make selection essential.

Different criteria are needed for archiving dynamic products, such as bibliographic databases or discussion forums. Snapshots are one suggestion here. These are versions, linked to date/time stamps. Some datasets require constant updating to maintain their value. Who has responsibility for ensuring the integrity of the updated material? For some non-cumulative databases where individual records are changed or deleted, it may be necessary to keep an audit trail of the changes made to a database over a period of time in order to preserve a comprehensive view of the data held.

1.5 How?

The need to manage the preservation of digital material both immediately and in the long term has encouraged the promotion of a wide range of approaches.

Should material be kept in a standard format or in its original format? Which is more important – functionality (what you can do with the information) or appearance (what it looked like)?

One approach – technology preservation – is to preserve both the original data and the platform necessary to interpret it. However, preserving digital objects in their original format and medium does not guarantee future usability, unless the particular technology on which they depend is also preserved and can be made to work over time.

Migration is the movement of digital objects from one technology to another. It is likely to be a continuous process, with material transferred to a series of new formats over time, and thus potentially an expensive option. In most cases migration is less of a problem from a hardware point of view than that of the software platform.

The technological options are described in more detail in chapter 4.

Cost management principles would suggest that digital material should preferably be held in archives in a standard format, on standard media, and managed by one of a few standard operating systems. Material that does not conform would either have to be processed prior to entering the preservation store or be managed under a different regime with a premium scale of charges.

However, prescriptive standards in the electronic information world have so far failed to achieve full recognition. The emphasis is now on 'permissive standards', such as Standard Generalised Markup Language (SGML), which do not tell document creators how to format the document or even what software should be used, but result in an environment that allows exchange of information.

Rather than a prescriptive approach, many of those involved in the creation and management of digital information would prefer to see the development of guidelines and guidance both for specific audiences and for specific types of material.

Certain best practices appropriate for digital preservation can be automated for data creators through the application software they use. This is particularly true with regard to data documentation and metadata, key elements of which can be generated automatically by application software as and when it is used. Accordingly, the development of appropriate software and tools may play a key role in digital preservation.

Prospects for and the costs involved in preserving digital resources over the longer term rest heavily upon decisions taken about those resources at different stages of their life-cycle. Decisions taken in the design and creation of a digital resource, and those taken when a digital resource is accessioned into a collection, are particularly influential.

1.6 Whose responsibility?

There are many groups and organisations with some degree of involvement in digital information; they are referred to in this report as *stakeholders*. They bring different perspectives to the need for digital archiving and digital preservation, and their interests are also different. While some are concerned purely with preservation, others are more interested in access to and re-use of material. For example, re-analysis of data is a central principle of scientific scholarship. Other groups are principally interested in commercial exploitation in the future.

Who are the stakeholders? Some of the groups that have been identified are: authors; libraries; publishers; archive centres; distributors; IT suppliers; legal depositories; consortia; and networked information service providers. We should also include industry and business amongst the stakeholders. For example, pharmaceutical companies need to keep records indefinitely and might be persuaded to contribute to research into preservation methods.

While many stakeholders are involved with data resources at different stages, few have influence over (or even interest in) those resources throughout their entire life-cycle. Organisations with a remit for long-term preservation, for example, acquire digital resources to preserve them and encourage their re-use but often have little direct influence over how they are created. This means that decisions which affect the prospects for and the costs involved in data preservation are distributed across a number of different (and often differently interested) groups.

Where should responsibility for digital archiving lie? At present there are few incentives to preserve data and few requirements to do so.

Responsibility for archiving falls naturally on the creator or owner of the information, who should understand how it works and what its value is. However, ownership of digital data is often unclear, and in these situations it is very difficult for organisations to develop preservation strategies. Ownership also brings other responsibilities, such as making sure that rights management issues and intellectual property are respected. There is a risk that some agencies may disclaim ownership in order to absolve themselves of responsibilities for preservation and liability. Others may use their ownership to prevent actions aimed at preservation for short term reasons.

If the initial creators or owners of digital information fail to meet their responsibilities, then some other organisation, such as a digital archive repository, would have to intervene; and legislation would be required for this.

Data creators who attach little or no value to the long-term preservation of the data resources they create (and these are currently in the majority) are unlikely to adopt standards and practices which will facilitate their preservation, especially where doing so would involve extra costs. We need to make them aware of the benefits of preservation in a manner which appeals to their interests.

Chapter 2 discusses more fully the rights and responsibilities of stakeholders, while chapter 3 suggests a policy framework to assist those involved in the creation and preservation of digital resources to formulate their own data policies.

1.7 Who pays? How much will it cost?

The widespread and growing use of digital objects means that their preservation is a general problem throughout society. Failure to preserve them adequately will damage future scholarship and weaken the cultural heritage.

But who should pay for digital preservation? Is the system for print publications – legal deposit through the British Library and other deposit libraries, suitable for digital archives? It is widely felt that digital archives should be funded by the government, ultimately by the taxpayer. An alternative approach might be for communities with a common interest to decide to fund digital preservation on a shared basis. Funding could be shared among various sources, with publishers, creators of information (including the academic community), libraries and users all making a contribution. Other possibilities include private sector involvement, funding by charitable trusts, as in the USA, and international collaboration through the European Union.

Should users pay fees for access? Or should it be free at the point of use? The possibility for generating income exists but is also unquantified.

Overall, digital archiving is a cost-unknown venture. We need to establish more precisely how much it will all cost, by constructing different working models based on different ways of doing it. Any strategy for long-term preservation must also take into account the possibility that the level of resources that may be devoted to digital archiving will not be available over the long term.

Chapter 5 discusses the costs involved in digital preservation and proposes a model that can be used to compare the costs of different methods of preservation.

1.8 Who has access?

Access involves both technical issues (ensuring that digital objects are maintained in a usable form) and legal issues (establishing ownership and protecting copyright). For an archive, a digital object must be technically accessible both when access is legally permitted and when it is not.

It is also a contentious issue. There seem to be two distinct groups involved, each with different motivations: those whose primary interest is access to digitised materials on as wide a scale and at the lowest cost possible; and those who want preservation with no, or very restricted, access. The challenge is to find a way of satisfying both groups.

What is needed is a series of generic rules on access that can be adapted by negotiation in specific cases. There is also likely to be a number of new operating arrangements, enabled by technology, to secure appropriate access.

A key issue is how to provide users with access to material while protecting the interests of copyright holders. Is 'fair dealing' possible with electronic publications? Can copyright apply to transient data? Several solutions have been suggested: providing recompense to the copyright holder for use while material is current; licensing arrangements; or the use of metadata to embed the details of the copyright holder in the document. IT mechanisms may also be deployed which ensure that unauthorised copying is impossible. For example, an Electronic Copyright Management System (ECMS) may produce a watermark, a mark embedded in a document which will show on all printouts to identify the publisher, even if the text is edited.

There remain problems, though, in establishing ownership of digital material. In many cases it is very difficult to identify exactly who is the rights holder. The enormous variety of agencies publishing and distributing digital objects, along with the numerous and ill-defined roles of the creators of digital objects, make for a confused and complex situation.

Apart from the fraught area of copyright, authors and owners of digital information have moral rights which must also be respected, including integrity (protection against corruption of the work), the right to be named as author, and protection against misattribution. It is not yet clear how moral rights will affect preservation.

Both users and owners of digital material require guarantees of security and authenticity; the assurance that, once archived, an item cannot be changed.

1.9 What kind of strategy?

At present, the short-term focus on cost-efficiency during data creation is dominant. It is up to relevant organisations to take an active role in publicising to other stakeholders the value of the long-term preservation of selected digital resources, and to demonstrate the benefits of any additional investment during data creation in terms of efficiencies and use later in the life-cycle of the resource.

Digital preservation remains relatively undeveloped. The UK lacks a strategy for the long term preservation of digital information on a scale sufficiently large to support future scholarship and research. A strategy for digital preservation is part and parcel of any national information policy and it should be integral to any investment in digital libraries and information superhighways. How should such a strategy be formulated? What form should it take?

The government has now accepted the principle that digital archiving should be subject to legislation in the same way as, or as an extension of, legal deposit for printed material. Without a legal deposit system it would be unclear how any authority would ensure that originators preserve their material, or make partnerships to preserve it. Even with such a system, there will still be many thousands of originators whose work is not 'published' and which therefore falls outside the scope of legal deposit legislation. It will be difficult to ascertain whether they are all preserving their material properly. As a fail-safe mechanism, archives could be given rights for 'aggressive rescue', where organisations were seen to be failing in their responsibilities, but policing such a system would be difficult and expensive.

Should the system be centralised or distributed? Centralised storage offers the benefit of economies of scale. However, a central body might be seen as a threat to the independence of existing agencies. Different archiving groups may be formed where there is common interest in preserving a cluster of information, as defined by the stakeholders.

The nature and scale of long-term digital preservation are such that no single agency is likely to be able to undertake the role of preserving all digital materials within its purview or the necessary research and development in this field. Cooperative agreements and consortia will be required. These will need to address a wide range of issues including, for example, the division of responsibility for different subject areas or materials, selection of material, the degree of redundancy which may be desirable for preservation or multiple locations for access, funding, and different national or regional needs.

Preservation is widely regarded as being for the common good, but there are high costs involved. What part will market demand play in deciding what will be archived? Should it be left to market forces alone? Can we harness market forces for the public good by making it economically rewarding to deposit data, to encourage people to comply as they realise the value locked up in their data? The Task Force on Digital Archiving, created in the USA by the Commission on Preservation and Access and the Research Libraries Group (Waters and Garrett, 1996), commented that:

'*Without the operation of a formal certification program and a fail-safe mechanism, preservation of the nation's cultural heritage in digital form will likely be overly dependent on marketplace forces, which may value information for too short a period and without applying broader, public interest criteria.*'

2 stakeholders: rights and responsibilities

2.1 Who are the stakeholders?

Many different groups have an interest or involvement in digital information. Any strategy for digital preservation will naturally have to take into account the various needs and perspectives of these groups. The stakeholders include:

- Authors
- Publishers
- Libraries
- Archive centres
- Distributors
- Networked information service providers
- IT suppliers
- Legal depositories
- Consortia
- Universities
- Research funders

Another way of identifying the stakeholders is by their main area of interest in relation to digital material. Using this method Table 1 lists ten stakeholders *(see right)*.

It is interesting to note that roles and interests may change over the long term. For example, copyright will lapse after a certain length of time: will this make it less attractive to the copyright owner to make a contribution to long term preservation?

A relative newcomer to the scene are the interferers. They may be seen as the antithesis of the regulators, although new regulations may be brought in to counter their activities. Sometimes they may simply be a nuisance, obstructing the course of good preservation practice, taking a narrow perspective on minor issues, or delaying the introduction of new measures. At other levels their effects may be far-reaching. Budget cuts, for example, can seriously damage the value of a collection, by restricting intake and causing holdings to be disposed of. Political instability can destroy centuries of preservation, the intellectual heritage of a culture.

Table 1: Stakeholders' interest and impact on the long term preservation of digital material

Stakeholder	Interest and impact on the long term preservation of digital material
Initiators	Collection development. Research libraries collect material that is current, published on current technology. Establish the nature and scale of the threat of irretrievable loss for digital material items.
Regulators	Legal deposit; Public Record Office; Copyright. Legislation to preserve ownership for a limited period of time, to ensure a national collection of material is established and to preserve items that are in the public interest.
Creators	Creation of digital records. Lack of control over format of deposited items leads to unmanageable diversity
Rights owners	Maintain copyright. Preservation of material may lead owners to demand copyright in perpetuity.
Fund-holders	Manage the funds available for preservation activity according to agreed priorities and service levels.
Providers (1)	Initial diversity of formats at publication complicated by new editions in new formats and on new media.
Readers	Access to material. Readers will demand material in current acceptable format for display and inclusion in new digital material.
Archivists	Conserve the archive, whilst preserving the items, and maintain the integrity of the deposited items.
Providers (2)	Provide new editions, which link into the new intellectual context through re-indexing and re-packaging.
Interferers	Make material inaccessible through technological turbulence or blocking publication.

This chapter explores the attitudes of the stakeholders to the preservation of digital data, in terms of both their needs and their responsibilities. It has been compiled from two reports: *Responsibility for digital archiving and long term access to digital data* (Haynes *et al.*, 1997), and *An investigation into the digital preservation needs of universities and research funders* (The Data Archive, 1998). The research for both reports was carried out through interviews, questionnaires and focus group meetings.

The various stakeholders have been divided into two large groups: those involved in the electronic publication cycle; and those involved in the research community. This somewhat arbitrary division is made to reflect each group's major area of interest. There is, of course, a certain amount of overlap between them. For example, individual members of the research community are often authors and sometimes publishers as well.

2.2 The electronic publication cycle

The model shown in Figure I *(see below)* **represents the electronic publication cycle and identifies the key players at each stage in the process.**

Figure I. The electronic publication cycle

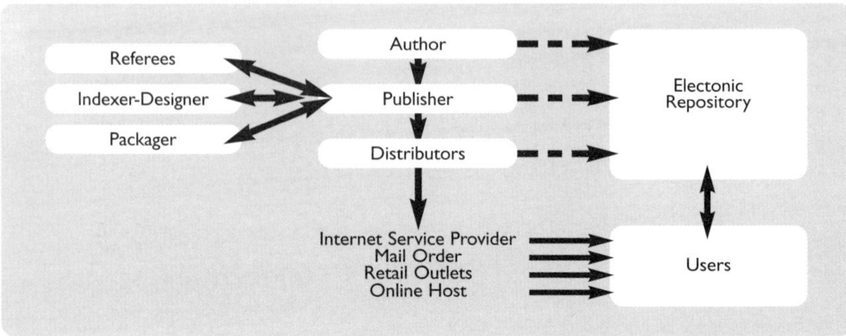

Table 2 shows the priorities and concerns of four of the major groups active in the publication cycle.

Table 2. Stakeholders' priorities and concerns

Rank	Authors, Data Originators	Publishers	Distributors	Repositories
1	Common strategic approach by providers of preservation services (coherence, consistency and interoperability).	Preservation of the functionality of electronic publications.	Criteria for permanent preservation. What is worth archiving?	Standards and common formats.
2	Intellectual property rights.	What constitutes a publication?	Contracts between archivists and information providers.	Permanence and refreshment of data.
			Co-operation between copyright holders to permit voluntary or legal deposit.	
3	Security (protecting against piracy; preservation against catastrophe; preservation of integrity – what is the authorative text?).	Who should keep digital materials? Rights holders' benefits. Who should pay?	Copyright issues.	Initial capture into an electronic record-keeping system.
4	Financial implications (Who pays? Who benefits?).	Need to use open standards in storing the data (e.g. SGML rather than Microsoft Word).	Funding and costs.	Access.
5	Migration and emulation from one generation to the next.	Rights owners' benefits.	How to organise all aspects of data emulation and migration.	Financial viability and responsibility.

Authors and data originators stress the need for a common strategic approach to archiving digital materials and (not surprisingly) for attention to intellectual property considerations, envisaging that the unilateral approach of libraries to decisions about preservation will have to give way to greater collaboration in future. They see national coordination of digital archives as a more appropriate way forward than a centralised national digital repository, hoping to allow groups with specific interests to manage their own archives whilst ensuring that material is more generally available. They feel that a common approach to archiving digital material entails providing a framework for guidelines (covering such issues as emulation and security as well as best practice in the area) which is not prescriptive, since otherwise it is likely to be ignored.

They see market demand as a major driving force in deciding what is to be archived and suggest that a voluntary approach, funded (at least initially) by the interested parties, might be more appropriate than asking for public funding for an unfocused national resource.

Publishers assume that a national archiving strategy based on the legal deposit libraries will emerge. Accordingly, they see a need to separate the repository function of bodies such as the British Library and their role of providing a document delivery service to make information more widely available. They see the British Library's Document Supply Centre as a commercial document provider which is, in effect, competing on unfair terms.

They feel that transfer of electronic publications could take place at the point of publication, as long as there are restrictions on release to the general public. If no guarantees can be made to protect publishers' commercial interests, the alternative would be to hand over the material at the point (defined by them) at which the publication is no longer of commercially exploitable value. While an electronic publication is commercially exploitable they feel that it is in the publishers' interests to maintain (and retain) it. (It should be perhaps be noted that this view is not shared by other groups who argue that this approach would leave some material vulnerable to neglect.)

Although publishers accept the idea of preservation for the common good, they argue that the humanistic goal of national collections being maintained and preserved as a service to scholarship is no longer tenable because of the large volume of material and high preservation costs involved.

Learned society publishers may take a different view from commercial publishers since they have always accepted a greater responsibility for meeting the needs of the intellectual community they represent. An archiving role may also be in their own interests.

The need to review the assumptions under which the deposit libraries operate is also highlighted by the ***distributors***. The question of who should make the decision about whether or not to archive an item will require collaboration between librarians, archivists, and publishers. They feel that it is unrealistic to depend on the publishers alone to ensure preservation of digital publications, even in the short term.

This group sees preservation and access as separate issues, whilst recognising that preservation only has a purpose if access is allowed to the material. However, they too accept the idea of preservation for the public good.

The group envisages various possibilities, from a systematic to an accidental approach. Taking a broad historical perspective, they argue that the sheer volume of digital material favours accidental preservation, with those items for which there is a continuous demand most likely to survive.

Although some types of digital publication, such as CD-ROMs, are seen as sufficiently coherent to be collected and archived, others, such as Internet sites, are not. Hypertext links present particular problems because of the difficulty of preserving the ability to link with other sites.

Contracts between archivists and information providers, as well as cooperation amongst copyright holders to permit voluntary or legal deposit, are seen as part of the necessary response to the breaking down of traditional divisions of functions between publishers and repositories.

Distributors question whether the collecting strategy of the past centuries, based on keeping every edition, is still relevant today. Whereas in the past the printing process was sufficiently laborious to ensure that publishing was relatively rare, electronic material can change so quickly that this approach may no longer be appropriate.

Predictably, the ***repositories*** take a somewhat different view of access and deposit issues. They suggest that in the future, preservation will require both an access copy and an archival copy of the data. The problem of legal deposit as it stands is that books on deposit are as accessible as any other book held. However, for electronic documents the same principle probably should not apply. They see the access and preservation roles becoming much more distinct for electronic documents.

They feel that the source of the data should determine how large data sets should be treated. Commercial publications should have strictly limited access with the emphasis on preservation. Public data (such as that coming within the remit of the Public Record Office) should be more widely available.

Repositories could save 'pointers' to the material while publishers maintain the actual archives (and at the same time exercise some control over access).

They acknowledge a 'heritage role' for digital archives, requiring access by the academic community.This is likely to lead to a number of new operating arrangements to secure appropriate access. For, example the British Film Institute has based its policy on the access role rather than purely on preservation, partly enabled by technology. The Data Archive has issued CD-ROMs of data for exclusive scholarly use and, where appropriate, proscribes use by commercially sponsored academics. This system depends on password access and undertakings by researchers not to use the data beyond agreed terms. A single-user licence could limit access to networks, but difficulties would remain over downloading of data and their subsequent exploitation.

When considering specific questions about the preservation of digital material the group as a whole offers a very diverse range of views.

Of the organisations contacted, three-quarters either have a policy on digital archiving, are working towards a policy, or feel that a policy is necessary. However, there is a also a perception that the responsibility for developing an archiving policy lies elsewhere, perhaps with an international or professional association, or through the requirements of legislation. Although some organisations have comprehensive policies in operation, others are strongly biased towards physical storage, with little consideration of access issues or migration to new media.

Views on who should be responsible for holding and archiving digital materials vary widely:

- A National Digital Repository, or variations on this theme, along with the appointment of a National Digital Preservation Officer. However, some doubt that a central repository would be able to fulfil the needs of all the different depositors.
- National libraries/legal deposit libraries/the British Library.
- The National Sound Archive is seen as a good example of a voluntary system of deposit.
- A system of distributed repositories, or a body to coordinate different repository agencies.
- Government, government departments or the public domain.
- Rights holders should be responsible for archiving their own material.
- Specialist agencies and those with historical responsibility for archiving.

Many representatives of this group see legal deposit as the most appropriate mechanism for ensuring that digital material is preserved, although there are fears about access and further thought is needed as to how the system would work in practice. Most agree that a voluntary code is unlikely to be satisfactory, although it could be useful initially until legislation is introduced.

Most also agree that once a digital object has been selected for preservation it should be kept forever, although some see that there are problems with the practicalities of this aspiration.

Opinions differ as to the format in which material should be kept. Some argue for the maintenance of digital materials in a standard format. Others express the view that archived material should be kept in its original format so as not to distort appearance or content. They suggest that any transformation or migration will lead to loss of data, but acknowledge that there are also problems in reading and accessing old technology.

The most common response to the question of funding is that it should be a national responsibility, funded by the government through taxation, although some feel that others have some role to play in funding: publishers, the creators of information (for example, the academic community), libraries, users.

Perhaps the greatest divergence of opinion is on access, with views ranging from the extremes of denying all access (i.e. material should be held purely for preservation) to making material freely available at no cost. Most agree that access should be allowed, but with restrictions, and that access and copyright should be subject to negotiation.

2.3 The research community

Electronic resources are being funded and created within the research community at an unprecedented rate, both in terms of data and of 'electronic paperwork'. The increase is due to the ubiquity of hardware and software, and the electronic infrastructure now available to researchers. The funding agencies are supporting projects which produce electronic materials. Large quantities of electronic materials are being created within UK universities. All of these are expected to increase.

There is now a growing concern that as more digital information is produced – much of it held only in digital form – it is essential to develop strategies for the selection and preservation of such material.

There is evidence to suggest that, although some representatives of the research community have a clear understanding and recognition of the importance of digital preservation, in the sector as a whole there is a lack of awareness of the need for preservation policies for electronic research materials. There are strong arguments for continuing to make digital information available, including: the need for scientific advances to build on what has gone before; principles of openness and replicability; making greater use of limited and expensive resources; and reducing the burden on respondents to surveys.

Many ***funding agencies*** report an increase in the number of projects creating electronic materials, and expect this trend to continue. As well as researchers within the university sector, some funding agencies also support individual researchers, in-house research, local authorities and school teachers. They also fund research in collaboration with other research agencies and with commercial companies, and these collaborations often go beyond national borders. Any policies for digital preservation will therefore have to accommodate the diversity of grant recipients as well as the variety of research carried out.

Examples of electronic data produced by research include: scientific experimental data; epidemiological data; social surveys; clinical trial data; metadata providing a description of metadata files; electronic teaching materials; musical and choreography notation; audiovisual files; and multimedia databases.

'Electronic paperwork' has increased the amount of electronic material available for preservation. Electronic mail, bulletin boards and mailing lists have become an important means of communication between academics. Funding agencies are also introducing systems to enable the online completion of grant applications. Hardware and software are being developed to meet an ever widening range of tasks: for example, in laboratory research many of the instruments used now produce an automatic electronic output.

Funding agencies agree that the electronic materials produced by researchers constitute a valuable resource and should be preserved. The reasons for preservation include making the best of resources through secondary analysis, for evaluation and replication of past research, and the investigation of scientific misconduct. There are some concerns, however:

- the independence and impartiality of the funding body could be compromised by secondary analysis;
- quality control over secondary analysis could not be guaranteed;
- respondent confidentiality and respect for the sensitivity of data could be placed in jeopardy;
- the security of preservation technologies (for electronic data) is suspect;
- sensitive or commercially valuable data might fall into the hands of unsuitable individuals or bodies.

Only a minority of funding agencies have established policies and/or guidelines regarding the preservation of electronic materials. The firmest of the policies are those of the Economic and Social Research Council (ESRC) and the Natural Environment Research Council (NERC). ESRC researchers are obliged to discuss data access at an early stage and to offer any electronic materials to The Data Archive at the University of Essex. NERC's policy is that grant recipients must satisfy the funder that they have the willingness, expertise and commitment to preserve data themselves or that they have made arrangements with an appropriate data centre to take responsibility for their data at a specified time point. While many research funders recognise the value of secondary analysis, ESRC is alone in actively encouraging secondary analysis over primary data collection.

Selection is one of the biggest problems. Limitations of resources mean that no archive can accept all material that it is offered. Materials preserved must include contextual information by which the materials can be understood and used correctly. The prediction of what will be useful in the future needs to be improved in order to avoid the accumulation of material of low value, and this will require an understanding of what constitutes value. Some datasets require constant updating in order to maintain their value and it is unclear who has responsibility for ensuring the integrity of the updated material.

There are also concerns about ownership. Ownership of electronic materials is rarely established clearly. Funded data collected by universities is the property of those universities and the research councils have no official authority over what happens to it, although they may exercise some unofficial leverage.

Ownership of data brings responsibilities in terms of access and preservation, although not all of the research funders who claim ownership accept the preservation of materials as their responsibility.

It is widely suggested that the creation of a culture of data sharing is needed, best achieved through a campaign promoting awareness of data preservation and its value. A statement of national policy and guidelines would enable agencies to be more confident in their requirements of researchers and would help to allay fears about the safety of materials once preserved, and the ease with which they can be located and accessed. Some agencies favour a centralised repository rather than a dispersed network, while others feel that a central body might threaten their independence. Most agencies agree that there should be national funding for the preservation of electronic resources, but not all feel able to make a contribution to such a fund.

There is extensive creation of digital materials by ***university research centres and projects***. These include: numerical data derived from experiments and surveys;

papers and reports in the form of text files; qualitative research data, such as interview transcripts and field notes; databases from historical sources; multimedia, audiovisual materials and World Wide Web pages; electronic tutorials and teaching materials; electronic mail messages; project administration files, agendas and minutes of meetings.

The sharing of electronic materials appears to be common within the academic sector. In most cases distribution is in the form of CD-ROM or over the Internet, particularly the World Wide Web, often through the production of specific gateways. Access to materials is most often achieved through informal agreements with the creators and copyright holders.

Many researchers agree that the re-analysis of data is a central principle of scientific scholarship and that secondary analysis can also bring cost benefits. On the whole they do not see a serious problem in predicting which digital materials are likely to be useful in the future. Nor do many consider that materials can only be fully understood by the original researcher, although they do recognise the difficulties involved in understanding other people's work.

Many researchers do not seem to know whether their funder has a policy regarding the preservation of the electronic materials they are creating, although most are strongly in favour of a policy being formulated. Some projects have their own internal preservation policies and some offer their materials to an archive, such as the Data Archive or an Arts and Humanities Data Service (AHDS) centre. The problems experienced when attempting to establish a preservation policy are:

- lack of national guidance
- lack of interest in out of date materials
- uncertainty about technical standards
- insufficient resources to carry out preservation.

Reasons for not archiving materials include: a lack of awareness about archives; the absence of archives suitable for the materials being created; the need for adequate metadata; and concerns about the legitimacy of lodging material in an external archive when the intellectual property rights are not clearly defined. In most cases the decision to deposit materials is dictated by the policy of the funding agency.

Many researchers consider the preservation of digital materials to be the joint responsibility of the projects generating the materials and the funding agencies. Ownership is a central concern. It conveys control, including the right and the responsibility to preserve the material; it is often closely linked to copyright; and it confers responsibility for ethical issues, accuracy and usability. In terms of funding, the general feeling is that fewer funds for primary research in order to fund preservation would be unacceptable, despite the cost benefits of secondary analysis in the long run.

In common with the funding agencies, many researchers favour a national body to advise on preservation policy and monitor all relevant developments in standards of best practice. A distributed network is also favoured to allow greater security and reliability, distribute work and storage capacity, avoid a monopoly situation, and allow for regional or discipline specific differences.

Although ***universities and higher education institutions*** (HEIs) are creating large and increasing quantities of electronic materials, none of the universities surveyed has established any procedures, policies or guidelines covering the preservation of electronic materials at their institutions. The reasons for this include insufficient resources to allocate to the task, lack of knowledge about electronic preservation, or conflicting priorities. In some cases the problem of data preservation has simply not been recognised.

Most vice-chancellors agree that the preservation of electronic materials should be a joint responsibility of researchers and the research funding agencies, although some see it as the remit of 'other organisations', such as the Higher Education Funding Councils' (HEFC) Joint Information Services Committee (JISC) and the British Library. Others stress the importance of flexibility, with the solution dependent on the nature of the electronic material. Again, ownership is seen as problematic; ownership of electronic materials is often unclear and digitisation exacerbates the problem of what constitutes intellectual property.

Questions of funding elicit a mixed response from vice-chancellors. Some suggest that preservation should be funded 'nationally' or 'centrally' from the public purse, or from HEFC funds, while others believe that the funding agencies should foot the bill. Other proposed sources include the private sector, and funds generated from commercial partnerships or from end users. Few believe that universities should pay for preservation directly, although some feel that their institution would be willing to contribute resources to it.

They agree that a national body responsible for advising on preservation policy would be useful, and favour expanding the role of an existing institution over the establishment of a brand new body, the most suitable candidates being the British Library, the National Preservation Office or the Consortium of University Research Libraries.

Vice-chancellors also suggest that a campaign to raise awareness of the problem of preserving electronic materials and a programme of education regarding preservation techniques would be useful. These should target a wide range of groups including the creators of digital materials, universities, publishers, database hosts, government departments, commercial organisations with a high level of involvement in research, central support services and research funders. This group also feels the need for a wider programme of research to tackle the range of political, legal and technical issues that remain unresolved.

Taking the research community as a whole, three main areas of concern are apparent:

- a lack of awareness of the need for preservation policies for electronic research materials;
- a need for advice, standards and national policy to plan for preservation;
- the need for a centre, or a distributed network of centres to provide preservation facilities for those without the facilities and resources to provide their own long-term preservation.

It is also clear that the form which centres of preservation should take and the responsibility for undertaking this work cannot be addressed until some serious issues have been debated and clarified. These issues centre on the link between ownership of the materials and the rights and responsibilities to preserve. The funding of research in the UK is very complex, making it impossible to draw a simple line between ownership and responsibility for preservation. Preservation is by its very nature a complex, expensive and, above all, a long-term commitment, while many research projects are short-term and shifting in funding, location and staffing. The potential value of the material they produce is inestimable, however, and in many cases its loss will be a loss to the nation's cultural and scientific heritage.

2.4 Conclusions

There is always a danger that surveys will over-represent those with an interest in the topic and that conclusions will be based on a self-selecting, unrepresentative minority, despite strenuous efforts to avoid this outcome. The views of non-respondents are likely to be just as interesting as the contributions of those who did participate – if only we could get at them. Nevertheless, it is possible to draw some broad conclusions about the perspectives on digital preservation of both communities.

1. There is concern across all sectors that resources are being lost and agreement on the need for a campaign to promote awareness of data preservation.

2. There is an acknowledgement of the role of the creators of digital information and their responsibility for its long-term preservation. This is linked to concerns about

the ownership of digital material and the protection of intellectual property rights.

3. There is common concern about the costs of preservation, especially since the scale of costs involved is an unknown factor.

4. There is no consensus, however, on how digital preservation might be financed, although many indicate that some form of national funding is necessary.

5. There is also agreement on the need for collaborative developments, and for shared and agreed policies.

6. All express the need for guidance – a national policy and guidelines covering preservation of electronic materials. Many feel that a central national body should lead on preservation policy and monitor all relevant developments in standards and best practice.

7. Overall there is a lack of established policies and guidelines and evidence to suggest that the majority of organisations have not thought through the implications of digital preservation. Clearly, there are exceptions to this, and it is to those organisations which have taken a lead that we must look for examples of best practice.

3 **encouraging** and learning from best practice

3.1 Different stakeholders, different interests

While the previous chapter examined the different views of the various stakeholders involved in digital information, this chapter takes another perspective and looks at the subject from the point of view of the life-cycle of the digital object itself. Different stakeholders become involved with data resources at different stages. Indeed, few organisations or individuals that contribute to the development and management of digital resources have influence over (or even interest in) those resources throughout their entire life-cycle. Data creators, for example, have substantial control over how and why digital resources are created, but few as yet extend that interest to how those resources are managed over the longer term. In some cases they cannot, particularly where resources are not available or allocated for this task. Organisations with a remit for long-term preservation, on the other hand, acquire digital resources to preserve them and encourage their re-use but often have little direct influence over how they are created.

The result is that digital preservation is essentially a distributed process, which engages a range of different (and often differently interested) stakeholders who become involved with digital resources at particular phases of their life-cycle. Although stakeholders have a clear understanding of their own involvement in digital resources, they have less understanding of the interests of others. Further, they may have little or no understanding of how their own involvement influences (or is influenced by) others, nor awareness of the current challenges in ensuring the long-term preservation of the cultural and intellectual heritage in digital form. To increase the prospects for digital preservation – and reduce its cost – different groups of stakeholders need to become more aware of how their particular involvement with a digital resource ramifies across its life-cycle.

In other words, we need to look at 'the big picture'.

3.2 Experience, cross-fertilisation and information-sharing

Some groups of organisations, including data banks, institutional archives and academic data archives, have long experience of managing data over the longer

term. The library and cultural heritage sectors have initiated further research and development in this area. Despite their different aims, and the different business, funding and legal environments in which they work, these stakeholders have a great deal in common; some have 30 years and more of highly relevant data management experience. Nonetheless, there are few channels to facilitate their inter-communication. Cross-fertilisation and information sharing are crucial to the success of long-term preservation. Particular attention should be paid to the experience of the data banks and the institutional archives, experience which is often overlooked in other current research and development activities.

The challenges posed by digital information are leading to a recognition of the inter-dependence between the stages of creation, use and preservation of digital resources, and the importance of the legal and economic environments in which they operate. As the digital store grows and diversifies we become more aware of the need for selection, standards and cooperation between different organisations.

All stakeholders acknowledge as essential the use of standards throughout the life-cycle of a digital resource. Their application ensures that data resources fulfil at minimum cost the objectives for which they were made. They also facilitate and reduce the cost of interchange across platforms and between individuals and institutions. The selection and use of standards, however, is highly contingent upon where in its life course any individual or organisation encounters a digital resource, and on the role which that individual or organisation plays in the creation, management, or distribution and use of the resource.

Little information is available about how a constellation of standards and methods may be applied effectively to a digital resource at various stages of its life-cycle in order to achieve very specific and clearly articulated aims. We need to identify and document such 'best practices' in order to provide integrated access to them in a meaningful way.

The complex inter-relationships between different practices involved in the life-cycle of digital resources have suggested the need for an integrated policy framework to develop a cost-effective approach to resource creation, preservation and use.

3.3 An integrated policy framework

The Arts and Humanities Data Service (AHDS) has developed a policy framework based on the concept of the life-cycle of a digital resource, with the aim of assisting those involved in the creation of and access to digital resources in identifying and

Table 3. Life-cycle of a digital resource.

1. Data creation	Decisions made when the digital resource was created – often outside the control of the collection manager, but having a major impact on the options subsequently available.
2. Data management and preservation	
Acquisition, retention or disposal	Decisions based on the digital resource's content, usability and relevance to users; the ease with which it can be managed, catalogued, made accessible and preserved.
Data structure	How a digital resource is formatted, compressed and encoded.
Data description and documentation	The extent to which the digital resourceís structure, content, provenance and history have been documented.
Data storage	The computer hardware and media used to store the digital resource.
Data preservation	Safeguarding the information content of any digital resource from the ravages of time, technological change and decaying magnetic media. Different strategies are appropriate for different data types and structures. Preservation requirements will impinge on how digital resources are structured, documented, stored and validated and possibly even on the conditions and methods by which digital resources can be accessed by end users.
3. Data use	Decisions on how digital resources are to be delivered and used; will be influenced by how they were created and will influence how they are managed.
4. Rights management	Intellectual property rights, data protection and confidentiality issues; need to develop both acquisition licences and distribution licences and implementation procedures.

addressing key issues and in developing their own data policies (Beagrie and Greenstein, 1998).

The framework outlines the main stages in the life-cycle of a digital resource, the role and functions of different generic stakeholders within this, and the inter-relationships between each stage against the implications for preservation of those resources designated of long-term cultural and intellectual value. It provides a high-level checklist which individuals and institutions can use to develop policies and guidance which they will tailor to their specific needs. In so doing they will also identify the implications across each stage, and the impact on, or made by, other players involved.The overall effect should be to provide policies and implementation strategies where the cost/benefits have been fully explored and strategic partners or dependencies identified.

3.4 The life-cycle of a digital resource

Table 3 *(see above)* summarises the main stages in the life-cycle of a digital resource.

All the key issues and all the elements of the framework are closely interrelated. Decisions about whether to create or include a digital resource in a collection – and about its content and format – will impinge on how it can be managed and stored, on how or even whether it can be preserved, and on how copies can be delivered to end users. Equally, the uses intended for a particular resource, or the method chosen to preserve it over time, should influence decisions taken when creating or including a digital resource in a collection.

The legal and economic environment surrounding the resource, interlinked with the organisational mission of its stakeholders, will also impact on the application of the framework. For example, the legal or contractual rights vested in a resource will impinge on how and whether it may be represented in machine-readable form; how, by whom, and under what conditions it may be used; how it can and should be documented and even stored; and how, whether, and by whom it can legally be preserved.

Similarly, resources created in a commercial environment may have commercial constraints which can impinge on data management, preservation, and use, while the priorities and objectives of funding, and the funding agencies, for the resource throughout its life-cycle may also impact in a number of different ways.

Some organisations have begun to implement proactive strategies to influence and manage the life-cycle of digital resources. 'Remote management' initiatives taken to manage 'active' or 'dynamic' resources or contract for specialist skills and facilities, appears to be a widespread response to a distributed process and best practice in its use should be developed and encouraged.

3.5 The framework in practice

The AHDS framework is supported by a number of case studies which provide a synthesis of existing practice, policies and implementation strategies. They introduce a range of stakeholders and organisational roles in the creation, management and preservation of digital resources.

Data banks, such as university computing services, perform large-scale data storage functions for a broad constituent community. They are contract data services whose core function is to act as 'safety deposit boxes' in which data creators deposit their data for safe keeping under some form of agreement, and from which depositors again may recall their data at some point in the future. The data bank ensures that deposited data are available on contemporary storage media and leaves depositors to worry about whether they can be represented on and meaningfully accessed with contemporary hardware and software. In some cases, the data bank may also contract with a depositor to take on certain functions which are more closely associated with an institutional or academic data archive, though these may be said to be additions to their core services. Examples of data banks include the Oxford University Computing Service (OUCS), which provides an archive for the electronic assets of the University of Oxford, and the University of London Computing Centre (ULCC), which acts as a data bank for a variety of depositors and offers a data bank facility for the UK Public Record Office's Computer Readable Data Archive.

'Digitisers' create data resources, or build collections of resources which are either created or acquired from third parties, for a variety of different but always very specific purposes. Space missions which install satellites for the purposes of transmitting digital images of space, archaeologists who build a simulated town plan of Pompeii, art curators who hang a virtual exhibition, and librarians who digitise images of printed books are all 'digitisers'. They exercise a substantial degree of control over the data creation process and their use of the framework is influenced by their focus on the particular purpose or purposes to which their data collections are to be put. The digitisers may be grouped in three broad categories which reflect their roles and their intentions in the data creation process:

- Research-oriented agencies and individuals create or acquire data resources in the course of (or as an output from) specific investigations.
- Library, archive, and cultural heritage organisations have existing collections made up predominantly of non-digital information objects. Their data creation and acquisition activities are guided by collection policies which govern the institution's curatorial work generally and focus on five main areas: collection management and accountability (e.g. through the creation of computer catalogues); collection development (e.g. by acquiring access to third-party data resources as a means of appropriately extending the institution's 'holdings'); access to the collections (e.g. through the creation and network delivery of digital surrogates for objects within the collection); preservation (e.g. through the creation of digital surrogates for at-risk objects within the collection); repair (e.g. through the creation of digital surrogates for fragile objects within the collection). It is likely that the organisational missions of this group will develop over time as the balance of collections moves towards objects in digital form and as those collections include an increasing proportion of accessions created as primary digital objects. At this point it is likely that this group will increasingly resemble other groups, such as academic data archives, which preserve and promote access to digital resources of long-term value. The current focus on the process of digitisation and the creation of surrogates in digital form will then be less dominant.
- Publishers produce primary or secondary data for commercial purposes. They are increasingly interested in exploiting the value of their back files.

Examples of digitisers include: among the research organisations, the Space Data Centre (SDC) at the Rutherford Appleton Laboratory; and, among the cultural heritage organisations and libraries, the British Film Institute (BFI), the National Museum of Science and Industry, and the Victoria and Albert Museum (V&A).

Funding and other agencies invest in the creation of digital information resources and sometimes exercise some strategic influence over the financial, business, and legal environments within which such resources are created. Positioned to determine how and why data resources are created, these agencies may have a determining role in whether, how, and at what cost data resources will be managed over the long-term, and made accessible for re-use. Their use of the framework may help to extend their influence over data resources throughout each stage of their life-cycle. Examples include the Natural Environment Research Council (NERC) and the Scottish Cultural Resources Access Network (SCRAN).

Institutional archives, such as government or business archives, selectively build and manage unique electronic records which are generated by an organisation and retained by that organisation to document its activities. They will also make deposited records available as required by the record-generating organisation. Institutional archives' use of the framework is governed by their involvement with unique records, their interest in those records' long-term retention, their influence, through the record-generating organisation, over the behaviour of data creators, and their reliance upon mandated deposit by those creators as a source of collection development. Examples include the Public Record Office (PRO) in the UK, and the Center for Electronic Records (CER) of the National Archives and Records Administration of the United States (NARA).

Academic data archives selectively develop, maintain, and encourage re-use of unique data resources which are of interest to particular end-using communities. The resources themselves are drawn from a wide variety of depositors, though once deposited, they typically become the curatorial responsibility of the academic data archive. The archives' use of the framework is influenced by their focus on secondary analysis, by their service to a specialist user community, by that user community's information requirements, and by their reliance upon voluntary or non-exclusive deposit as a means of collection development. Examples include the Data Archive, at the University of Essex, and the Arts and Humanities Data Service (AHDS).

Legal deposit libraries have an obligation to maintain and provide access to non-unique information objects whose deposit is legally prescribed and enforced upon producers of certain classes of those objects. Legal deposit libraries may supplement these core holdings through voluntary deposit and, funding permitted,

Table 4: A data bank: University of London Computing Centre (ULCC)

Stage in Life-Cycle	ULCC
Data creation	
Acting on a contract basis to manage data at the bit-stream level, with no interest in a data resource's future usage, and compelled for economic advantage to offer the same service to all, the data bank has little interest in how, why, or for whom deposited data are created.	This unique perspective is apparent in the core services offered at ULCC which accessions and stores data created in a variety of different standard and non-standard formats. Where ULCC's work with the PRO is concerned, PRO guidelines pertaining to the management of computer-readable datasets mitigate to a large extent the need for that role being taken up by the data bank.
Data acquisition	
The data bank operates on a cost for quantity economic model and so its role in data selection is limited.	ULCC departs some way from this norm in its work for the PRO. Although ULCC must archive all data resources and information systems deposited by the PRO, it does exercise some influence, in discussion with the PRO about accessioning priorities and costs, and with officials in government departments who are responsible for identifying and preparing records for long-term retention.
Structure and storage	
Data banks leave responsibility for how data are formatted, encoded and compressed with depositors, though may regulate how (e.g. on what media) deposited data may be transferred. They are therefore largely unconstrained in the data structures they can accommodate and will not normally need to restructure data unless they are contracted by the depositor to perform content migration or data distribution functions or to provide access services.	ULCC will undertake these additional functions when engaged (and funded) to do so either by the record-generating project, or by the designated University authority which may take responsibility for the long-term preservation of certain data resources. Government departments take account of data resources' physical and technical characteristics when selecting data for deposit. ULCC will also restructure data deposited by the PRO since it is engaged to migrate them through changing technical regimes and make them accessible to users.
Data description and documentation	
With the exception of essential administrative information which is supplied by the data bank to locate, name, and record other vital statistics about deposited data, data documentation is left entirely to the depositor.	Again, ULCC's role is exceptional where PRO data are concerned, since the PRO has contracted out to it some functions in standardising and enriching documentation that is supplied by depositors.
Data preservation	
Data banks migrate data files through storage media to ensure their readability, but content migration (ensuring that data can be meaningfully represented by and accessed from contemporary platforms) is the responsibility of the depositor. The data bank will rely upon extensive computing infrastructure which may include large-scale computer servers, robotic tape libraries, etc. Preservation is based around the management of archive copies of the deposited data resources; that is, copies which are independent of any online representation they may have.	*A preservation scenario:* Archive copies are stored on industry standard digital tape or other approved media as may arise, and there will be multiple copies of any single data file, some stored on and others stored off site, preferably in temperature controlled and fire-proof safes or rooms. Off-site copies should be a safe distance from on-site copies to ensure they are unaffected by any natural or man-made disaster affecting the on-site copies. Archive copies may be written with different software to protect data against corruption from malfunctioning or virus- or bug-ridden software, and may be made to comparable magnetic media purchased from different suppliers to guard against faults introduced by the media's suppliers into their products or into batches of their products. Data files stored as archive copies will be migrated periodically to new media with that migration taking place within a minimum time which reflects the media supplier's estimate for the media's viability under prevailing climatic conditions. In addition, media will be checked periodically for their readability. Such checking may be conducted automatically by archive systems according to parameters set by system operators. The integrity of data files may also be checked using checksum and similar procedures which may be implemented automatically by the archive system according to parameters set by system operators.

Stage in Life-Cycle	**ULCC**
Data use	
Beyond ensuring that depositors can recall their data on readable media, the data bank is unconcerned with re-use. User support is oriented exclusively toward depositors (typically also the data's sole users) and may include documentation about the service on offer, how it works, and how access to it may be acquired.	ULCC's position is complicated by its having been contracted to the PRO to distribute holdings in its Computer Readable Data Archive, and in this respect, to adopt functions more typically associated with an institutional or academic data archive. User support services are also complicated by the data bank's involvement in providing third-party access to PRO-deposited data.
Rights management	
Since the data depositor tends to be the sole user of data which are stored in a data bank, rights management is not a central concern.	Depositors take full responsibility for data they deposit in the archive.

through acquisition of objects either through subscription or purchase. Their use of the framework is governed by their reliance upon mandated deposit, their lack of influence over depositors' behaviour, and their orientation toward long-term preservation and secondary use. Examples include most national libraries.

3.6 Two case studies

Two organisations with interests in digital preservation are described here as examples of how key issues have been approached in practice and how different organisational missions shape approaches to the creation and preservation of digital resources.

The University of London Computing Centre (ULCC) fulfils the core functions of a ***data bank (see Table 4, above and previous page).*** It also acts under contract to the UK's Public Record Office (PRO) as the repository for some of the electronic records and information systems created by UK government departments and selected for long-term retention by the PRO. As a data bank, ULCC is principally responsible for preserving archived data at the bit-stream level. Additionally the ULCC is contracted by the PRO to distribute those data physically to secondary users (i.e. by transferring them on some magnetic media or via file transfer protocol (ftp)) and to make at least some of them accessible online. In these respects its involvement with PRO data takes on some of the characteristics associated with an institutional archive.

As a ***funding agency***, the Natural Environment Research Council (NERC) invests in data-producing scientific research and thus in the creation of data resources which are unique, expensive to create, difficult to reproduce, and of substantial value for scholarly re-use ***(see Table 5, opposite)***. Recognising that its investments in data-producing research may be maximised by guarding the longevity

Table 5. A funding agency: the Natural Environment Research Council (NERC)

Stage in Life-Cycle	NERC
Data creation	
The funding agencies use their money, and the application process through which it is distributed, to influence how and why data are created and to determine their subsequent disposition and use. They are positioned to fund only those which promise data which are: (a) fit for the purpose for which they are intended; (b) created according to appropriate standards and best practices; (c) useful and re-usable; and (d) manageable over the longer term. The extent to which the funding agencies prescribe content and technical criteria varies in part owing to the range and nature of the data resources they are interested in funding. Given their interest in data resources over their entire life-cycle, the adoption of standards and best practices are possibly even more important to the funding agencies than to the digitisers. These are considered in the development of funding agency data policies and in the evaluation of grant applications.	NERC has adopted data policies which determine the life-course of grant-funded data from their inception, through to their creation, management, and subsequent use. NERC expects of its grant applicants the rigorous evaluation of both content and technical criteria that is conducted by other digitisers when planning a data creation initiative. As added insurance against its data resources' futures, it may require successful grant applicants to work closely with an appropriate data centre in the creation of the data resources so as to ensure that such resources can be managed by that centre over the longer term. In terms of content and technical criteria, NERC cannot be too prescriptive since it is funding research in a wide range of scientific disciplines. Because it funds the development of a wide range of data resources which are created for very different purposes, NERC is not prescriptive, relying upon specialists involved in the application review process to advise about appropriate use of standards and best practice.
Data management and preservation	
Funding agencies take a serious interest in how data are managed and preserved because they recognise the long-term scholarly value of the research resources created by their grantholders.	Decisions about how to store, document, and preserve grant-funded data are contingent upon the nature of the data and upon the practices of the NERC data centre or institution where they are ultimately managed. Broadly, documentation standards which NERC may require from its grant holders are designed and implemented by the data centres with secondary users' information needs in view. The documentation pays particular attention to users' needs to assess quickly whether a data resource is appropriate for any analysis they intend. With regard to data storage, data will typically be managed in the format in which they were created. Where restructuring takes place, it does so to facilitate preservation or improved user access. With regard to preservation procedures, NERC relies upon its data centres which are well (though differently) equipped and which implement procedures akin to those apparent at the data banks and the institutional archives.
Data use	
Here, the funding agencies may have two roles: a specific one which entails encouraging the use or re-use of the data resources created by their grant-holders; and a general one which entails promoting awareness of the scholarly and other advantages which may accrue from the collection, professional management, and re-use of such resources.	For NERC, both roles are undertaken through the data centres, though in conformance with NERC's data policy which is written in part with reference to the transforming effect that the availability and use of high-quality data resources may have on research into aspects of the natural environment. Practices vary across the data centres, reflecting their diverse holdings and the different specialist user communities that each centre serves. In these respects, the data centres resemble academic data archives. Across the centres, data are distributed or made accessible to users through a variety of means which include the Internet and a range of portable magnetic media, with a range of supporting materials which reflect the information requirements of the data centres' respective specialist communities, and the kinds of data which are being supplied.

Stage in Life-Cycle	NERC
Rights management	
The funding agencies may manage rights as a means of further enhancing their influence over the life cycle of data resources produced by their grant holders.	The intellectual property vested in any data resources that are created by NERC employees are owned by NERC itself, enabling the funding agency to determine their future disposition and use. Where data resources are created by NERC-funded third parties (e.g. university-based academic staff), intellectual property resides with the third party (e.g. the host University) but NERC may attach, as a condition of grant, a clause requiring that any such data are deposited with a designated NERC data centre and that that centre be given a non-exclusive licence to distribute them for educational use. NERC also takes pains through user licences and other procedures to ensure that appropriate educational re-use is made of NERC-funded data resources many of which have potential for commercial exploitation. Although misuse is difficult to detect, NERC carefully vets applications for data access and is prepared to take action against users caught in transgression of the user licence.

of the data and by encouraging their re-use, NERC has developed a data policy which, with the aid of high-level institutional and financial commitment, governs the disposition of NERC-funded data and acts to ensure their availability over the longer term. It has also designated a range of data centres, which receive funding directly from the NERC and act as repositories (academic data archives) for data created with NERC funding.

3.7 Using the framework

The framework provides strategic guidance to stakeholders involved with digital resources at various stages of their life-cycle. Although its aim is to facilitate awareness about practices which may enhance the prospect for, and reduce the cost of, digital preservation, it is useful for anyone involved in the creation, management, and use of digital resources.

To implement the framework, stakeholders are recommended to assess the issues pertaining to them, but also to understand how their approach to those issues may have ramifications for the data resources which come under their remit and for other stakeholders who have been or may become involved with them at other stages of their life cycle.

The framework is particularly relevant to the costs involved in preserving digital resources. Decisions taken throughout the life-cycle of the resource, especially at the design and creation stage, will have implications for preservation costs. The framework therefore underpins the cost model developed by Cimtech, which is discussed in chapter 5.

4 technological decisions

4.1 What is involved in preserving digital resources?

Preservation is concerned with ensuring the longevity of a digital resource through changing technological regimes with a minimum loss of the resource's intellectual content. Since the format and functionality of a resource in a particular computer environment contribute to its intellectual content, there is more to preservation than simply 'preserving the information', whether that information is expressed as a set of images, a textual document, or a multimedia document.

Three main approaches to digital preservation have been developed:

- Preserve the original software (and possibly hardware) that was used to create and access the information. This is known as the technology preservation strategy. It also involves preserving both the original operating system and hardware on which to run it.
- Program future powerful computer systems to emulate older, obsolete computer platforms and operating systems as required. This is the technology emulation strategy.
- Ensure that the digital information is re-encoded in new formats before the old format becomes obsolete. This is the digital information migration strategy.

These three approaches are described in more detail below.

Those involved in digital preservation must handle a wide range of digital resources and these will influence their choice of digital preservation strategy. Some strategies are more suited than others to preserving a particular resource – the choice of strategy must reflect fitness for purpose. Table 6 *(see over)* lists ten generic digital resource categories and their characteristics. It is not a definitive grouping, but a selection of the common digital resource categories which those involved in the creation of and access to digital material are likely to encounter.

Certain technical factors will also impact on the choice of strategy for each category of resource: the basic data types employed in each category; the application programs used to create them; the structures applied to them; and the systems used to manage or distribute them prior to deposit.

4.2 Technology preservation

Being able to replicate the behaviour of a program and the look and feel of a document or publication has to be balanced against the costs and the technical difficulties that would be faced by anyone trying to keep ageing computer hardware platforms running.

Already in the brief history of computing, hundreds if not thousands of old proprietary computer hardware platforms have disappeared without trace. Today we are seeing the increasing dominance of a few computer platforms and, in theory, this should simplify the task of preserving them in future. However, even here there are difficulties, given the rapid obsolescence of computer components. It is unlikely that components for today's PCs could be sourced in ten years' time.

In general, this strategy can only be regarded as viable for the short to medium term, as a relatively desperate measure in cases where valuable digital resources cannot be converted to hardware and/or software independent formats and migrated forward. This would usually be due to the complexity of the digital resource and the fact that it was created on a proprietary and obsolete application program. Any collection manager in charge of a large collection of digital resources who relied solely on this strategy would very soon end up with a museum of ageing and incompatible computer hardware.

4.3 Technology emulation

This strategy involves designing emulator programs on current and future computer platforms and programming them to mimic the behaviour of old hardware platforms and to emulate specific operating system software. It requires extremely detailed specifications for the outdated hardware and operating system software. A less comprehensive approach might be to emulate specific data operations as, for example, programs set up to read obsolete world processing formats and display the information.

In general, emulation is a specialist strategy, where the need to maintain the look and feel of the original digital resource is of great importance to the users of the collection. As with technology preservation, it would be used in cases where digital resources cannot be converted into software independent formats and migrated forward.

Anyone relying solely on this strategy could be taking a significant risk. They would be depending on the technical ability of the software engineers to emulate a specific environment and sustain it, and on the commercial viability of anyone providing such a service.

Table 6. Categories of digital resource

Category of digital resource	Data types included in resource	Applications used to create/manage/distribute digital resource	Notes
1. Data sets	Alphanumeric data	Wide range of data processing applications; bespoke software and application packages; managed in flat file; networked; hierarchical; relational and object oriented databases; presented via presentation graphics, modelling software, report writers, etc.	Survey data; results of experiments; transaction data; event data; administrative data; attribute data; bibliographic data
2. Structured texts	Alphanumeric data; mark-up data; tags to other data types (raster and vector graphics)	Word processing; text editing; HTML editors; desktop/corporate publishing; LaTeX; SGML and application specific Document Type Definitions; XML	Literary texts; formal documents; corporate publications; commercial publications; Web pages
3. Office documents	Alphanumeric data; mark-up data; raster and vector graphics	Word processing; spreadsheets; document image processing; office suites; groupware; document management systems; relational databases	Sets of digital documents; Digitised paper images; links/ bundles created via office suites; groupware; HTML
4. Design data	Vector and raster graphics; alphanumeric data	CAD; word processing; document image processing; relational data-bases; object oriented databases	Product data; as built drawings; Models; plans
5. Presentation graphics	Vector/raster graphics; moving graphics alpha-numeric data; full motion video; interleaved audio and video	Business graphics; clip art; creative graphics; presentation systems; Computer Based Training; multimedia	Business presentations; formal courseware; CBT packages
6. Visual images	Raster graphics; alphanumeric data	Image capture software; image processing and editing software; object oriented; relational and flat file databases	Fine art; picture libraries; photographic libraries; medical images; images of historic/ manuscript documents
7. Speech & sound recordings	Audio data; MIDI; metadata	Speech processing; audio recording and playback; symbolic music recording; relational and flat file databases	Music libraries; sound effects; radio broadcasts; sound recordings; media
8. Video recordings	Digital video; full screen, full motion video; interleaved audio and video; metadata	Digital video frames stored as bitmaps; audio files; audio/video interleaved; compression systems; Relational & Flat File Databases	Media libraries; training centres; video clips games
9. Geographic/ mapping data	Vector and raster graphics; alphanumeric data	GIS systems; mapping software; relational & object oriented databases	Maps; coordinates; range of overlay data; links between data types
10. Interactive multimedia publications	Interleaved audio and video data; moving graphics; vector and raster graphics; alpha-numeric data	Authoring software; editing software; access software	Electronic publishing; educational and training material; marketing material; games etc

4.4 Digital information migration

Behind this strategy is the assumption that it is only worth preserving digital information if you can access it on current computer hardware and software platforms. As those platforms change, so collection managers must migrate their digital resources forwards to ensure that they remain accessible on the new platforms.

According to the Task Force on Digital Archiving (Waters and Garrett, 1996), migration is not optional – it is an essential operation, given the fact that the computer operating environments of digital archives will inevitably change over time.

There are a variety of migration strategies, appropriate to different formats of digital materials. The Task Force makes the point that no single strategy applies to all formats and none of the current preservation methods is entirely satisfactory.

A basic migration strategy involves ***changing media*** – transferring digital resources from less stable to more stable media. The simplest version of this strategy involves moving information from fragile magnetic media to more stable, controlled environments. A more extreme version would involve printing digital information onto paper or recording it on preservation quality microfilm. While this preserves a copy of the basic data, it destroys the digital functionality of the resource. Much valuable data – for example, computation capabilities, graphic display or indexing – will be lost in the process. It is impossible to microfilm the equations embedded in a spreadsheet, to print out an interactive full motion video, or to preserve a multimedia document as a flat file. Changing media should therefore be regarded as a last resort if no other strategy meets the requirements.

A second migration strategy relies on popular application software having ***backward compatibility***. The latest versions of most popular word processing packages are capable of decoding files created on earlier versions of the same package. Migration involves testing the process, loading files into the new version and saving them in the new file format.

However, this strategy cannot be relied upon over the long term or for more complex digital resources. No one software supplier is in control of all the technical or commercial factors needed to guarantee the continued viability and support of their application software. They may go out of business, or introduce a totally new software package and drop support for their old package.

The third migration strategy relies on ***interoperability*** between rival popular application programs. Digital resources created on one application program can be exported in a common interchange format and then imported into a rival application program without the need to run the specific program that was used to create them.

If such interoperability could be guaranteed between all the major competing application programs, then digital information migration would be a much easier process! The list of migration options would be endless.

Today, similar software can, at least partially, interpret files created by a different software package. However, even with simple digital resources the interchange is likely to involve some loss of data. For example, word processing programs allow authors to save work as simple alphanumeric text using the American Standard Code for Information Interchange (ASCII) or other interchange formats such as Rich Text Format (RTF). Documents are rarely pure text – they also include format data, figures and footnotes, which may be lost in the interchange.

The more complex the digital resource, the greater the potential loss is likely to be. For example, interchanging the data held in geographical information systems (GIS) databases and groupware databases could involve the loss of thousands of links that have taken years of effort to create and which represent the bulk of the value of the database.

A fourth migration strategy – ***conversion to standard formats*** – is particularly appropriate for digital archives with large, complex, and diverse collections of digital materials. It proposes an enhanced version of the interoperability strategy. Where the latter relies on interchange formats that can be generated automatically from within applications, with this strategy the onus is placed on collection managers to define the preferred formats and select those that are most appropriate for the digital resources they collect and the users they serve.

The aim is to migrate digital objects from the great multiplicity of formats used to a smaller, more manageable number of standard formats that can still encode the complexity of structure and form of the original. For example, a digital archive might require that textual documents conform to standards such as SGML, or that images conform to a Tagged Image File Format (TIFF) format and standard compression algorithms.

The formats chosen for conversion will be determined by the structure of the digital resources themselves, the objectives set by the collection manager, and users' requirements. For example, the decision will be influenced by whether priority is given to preserving the ability to process or edit the digital resource, or to preserving its format or visual presentation.

For example, in many data centres a key objective is to preserve and make the data available in a format which allows them to be loaded into user application programs, processed and new data derived from them. The content is the valuable resource, while its presentation is of secondary importance. In archives and records centres, on the other hand, the priority may well be to preserve the format or visual presentation of the digital resource, in order to ensure its archival integrity.

While digital information migration is widely adopted, as a strategy it is still evolving. Techniques should become more effective as practical experience grows, but it remains largely experimental. Further research and development efforts are required to test the technical feasibility of the various approaches over the long term. However, since most migration strategies have the potential to lose information, a copy of the original bitstream should be preserved in all cases. This may later turn out to contain important clues lost or corrupted in the migration process.

4.5 Selecting the most appropriate long term preservation strategy

The best preservation strategy for *data sets* is conversion to standard formats. Some data sets are created in a 'controlled' environment, following professional standards for the production of formal interchange documents, or standard templates and house styles. If this is not the case, and the data are incomplete or lack adequate documentation, the archive may have to spend time and resources processing the data in order to make them usable.

The best approach to preserving data sets is for the archive to set standards and provide guidance for depositors, stipulating how records should be structured for deposit. The Research Councils – for example, the Natural Environment Research Council (NERC), described in the previous chapter – are beginning to adopt this approach, making it the responsibility of depositors to document their data sets fully and to deposit them in an appropriate format.

Most archives which specialise in the preservation of ***structured texts*** have adopted the digital information migration strategy, especially conversion to standard formats. The Oxford Text Archive (OTA), for example, follows the Text Encoding Initiative (TEI) guidelines for using SGML to mark up literary works. There are different versions of TEI for different categories of literary work; OTA uses TEI Lite as a basic standard. Increasingly, regular depositors are themselves adopting TEI Lite.

In some cases deposited texts may have been created using a proprietary desktop publishing application or management system. If these became obsolete then the archive might need to preserve the operating environment that they ran on before developing a migration strategy that allowed conversion to a standard format.

Office documents may be created in a variety of data types. The Public Record Office (PRO) draft guidelines address the long-term storage of electronic records created on office systems and recommend the digital information migration strategy, specifically conversion to standard formats. The formats they recommend are PostScript, Adobe's Portable Document Format (PDF), TIFF, SGML, and Comma Separated Variable ASCII for alphanumeric data. The PRO endorses strategies in which the format and presentation of the document are preserved as well as its content.

The PRO also identifies a potential problem with proprietary applications where, for example, vital attribute data and links between the documents might be held in an office suite application, groupware database or document management system. In this case it would be necessary to preserve the operating environment that they ran on until the links could be captured in a standard form.

Design data are made up of many data types: vector graphics (computer aided design); raster graphics (old manual drawings); and alphanumeric data (text documents plus attribute data in databases). They may be held in two and three-dimensional formats.

Archives which manage this category of digital resource recommend the digital information migration strategy and make use of a combination of backward compatibility, interoperability and conversion to standard formats. For interchange they tend to rely on the de facto DXF format, or Initial Graphics Exchange Specification (IGES) for two and three dimensional vector graphics. Standard formatted forms include HPGL; Encapsulated PostScript and TIFF.

Presentation graphics may comprise vector graphics (CAD), raster graphics, animation (moving graphics), and alphanumeric data. The digital information migration strategy is appropriate here, using a combination of backward compatibility, conversion to standard formats and changing media. Standard formatted forms include PostScript; Adobe PDF and TIFF. Technology preservation or technology emulation would only be employed where valuable presentations had been left on a proprietary platform which was now obsolete and where valuable data would be lost in translating the data to a standard format.

Visual images comprise one main data type – raster graphics data. In addition, alphanumeric data relating to the images may be held and managed in a database. Most archives which specialise in the preservation of visual images have adopted digital information migration, specifically conversion to standard formats. Those who are involved in preserving visual images must also make decisions on resolution, file formats, compression, and whether the images should be captured as black and white, greyscale, or colour.

For the very specialised area of ***speech or sound recordings*** the digital information migration strategy is suitable, using a combination of backward compatibility, conversion to standard formats and changing media.

Digital speech processing can be divided up into three areas: speech coding (the analogue-to-digital conversion of speech signals or waveforms, the compression of the digital signals, and the reverse digital-to-analogue conversion for play back purposes); speech synthesis (the translation by computers of a coded description of a message into speech, i.e. computers 'talking'); and speech recognition and understanding, which facilitate people 'talking' to computers, dictating text or issuing commands. Sound coding involves the analogue-to-digital conversion of sound signals, the compression and/or storage of the digital signal, and the reverse digital-to-analogue conversion for play back purposes. Any sound, including speech and music, can be recorded in this way. Music can also be described in a symbolic way – we have used printed musical scores for centuries. For computer systems the Musical Instrument Digital Interface (MIDI) standard defines how to code all the elements of musical scores, including notes, timing conditions, and the instruments to play each note. The sound files which are to be preserved will generally contain sound data coded either as a digitised analogue sound signal or as notes for a MIDI instrument.

Digital video recordings, another very specialised area, involve one main data type – motion video or moving image data. Increasingly, digital video resources contain interleaved audio data as well. Alphanumeric data relating to the moving images or interleaved audio and video data may also be held and managed in a database. The preservation of digital video data is still in the early stages and the bulk of holdings are likely to be in analogue film or videotape formats. Where practical, archives have adopted the digital information migration strategy, especially conversion to standard format. The Motion Picture Experts Group (MPEG) standards provide several standards for the compression of full motion video.

This is an area where early digital video material was created on proprietary applications and held in proprietary formats. Where the applications are now obsolete, a technology preservation or technology emulation strategy may be needed as a temporary measure to preserve the data.

Geographic/mapping data can cover almost all data types, including raster graphics, (base mapping data), vector graphics, and alphanumeric data held in databases. Geographic data can be held in two and three-dimensional formats. Cartographic software packages range in sophistication and functionality from atlases and route planners up to full geographical information systems (GIS). For this category of digital resource the digital information migration strategy is recommended, using a combination of backward compatibility, interoperability and conversion to standard formats as appropriate, with changing media as a back-up option.

By definition ***multimedia*** publications involve at least three data types. Most contain motion video with audio data interleaved; many comprise animation with interleaved audio data; and many will also involve some still images, graphics and alphanumeric data. Most early multimedia publications were produced on one of the compact disk (CD) formats and will have been authored and edited using proprietary multimedia editing and authoring packages. They will be accessed via proprietary access software. A strategy of technology preservation or technology emulation may be the best way to preserve the data until a practical migration strategy is developed. It may prove difficult to migrate the data in future without the loss of considerable data.

This is a very specialised and still relatively new area where individual studies need to be conducted by experts in the field who appreciate the specific challenges and risks which a migration strategy pose to interactive multimedia publications. They probably represent the most difficult category of digital resource to preserve today.

Table 7 *(see below)* provides a summary of digital resources and the preservation strategies recommended for them.

Table 7. Summary of digital resources and their recommended preservation strategies

Digital resource	Preservation strategy	Subset of strategy	Notes
1. Data sets	Digital Information Migration	Conversion to Standard Formats	
2. Structured texts	Digital Information Migration	Conversion to Standard Formats	
3. Office documents	Digital Information Migration	Conversion to Standard Formats, Backward Compatibility, Change Media	
4. Design data	Digital Information Migration	Backward Compatibility, Interoperability, Conversion to Standard Formats, Change Media	Technology preservation/ emulation as short term strategy for product data on obsolete systems.
5. Presentation graphics	Digital Information Migration	Backward Compatibility, Conversion to Standard Formats, Change Media	
6. Visual images	Digital Information Migration	Backward Compatibility, Conversion to Standard Formats, Change Media	
7. Speech & sound recordings	Digital Information Migration	Backward Compatibility, Conversion to Standard Formats, Change Media	A specialised area where additional work is needed by experts in the field.
8. Video recordings	Digital Information Migration	Backward Compatibility, Conversion to Standard Formats, Change Media	A specialised area where additional work is needed by experts in the field. Technology preservation/ emulation needed in short term where data locked in proprietary systems.
9. Geographic/ mapping data	Digital Information Migration	Backward Compatibility, Interoperability, conversion to standard formats.	A specialised area where additional work is needed by experts in the field. Technology preservation/ emulation needed in short term where data locked in proprietary systems.
10. Interactive multimedia publications	Technology preservation/ emulation in short term for data in proprietory systems until agreed strat-egies can be developed.		A specialised area where additional work is needed by experts in the field.

5 **estimating** the costs of digital preservation

5.1 Isolating a 'preservation cost'

Deciding on the techniques for preservation is only part of the picture. A key question for everyone interested in digital preservation is – how much will it cost? One of the problems encountered in trying to answer this question is that all the aspects and tasks involved in digital collection management are closely interlinked, making it very difficult to identify those elements which relate solely to preservation. For the same reason, it is difficult to isolate that portion of a data centre's budget which is concerned only with preservation. Some costs do relate specifically to preservation, but this does not mean that those are the only costs incurred when preserving digital resources. For example, does the cost of creating an online catalogue or a printed catalogue count as a preservation cost?

Rather than attempting to isolate a global preservation cost, we should assume that there are some preservation costs associated with all the elements involved in the life-cycle of a digital resource.

5.2 A cost model

Cimtech has developed a cost model that can be used to establish and compare the costs of the preferred methods of preservation for each category of digital resource (Hendley, 1998). It is based on the integrated policy framework drawn up by AHDS, which was described in chapter 3. It defines seven key areas, based on the life-cycle of the digital resource, which must be addressed by any digital collection policy, of which preservation is one. Given that a successful preservation strategy depends upon good practice in all the other six areas in the framework, the cost model also needs to take into account the costs incurred in each of those other six areas. The seven areas are:

1. Data creation
2. Data selection and evaluation
3. Data management, including:
   Data documentation
   Data validation, including:
      Data assessment
      Data copying
      Media refreshment

Data structure
Data storage

4. Resource disclosure
5. Data use
6. Data preservation
7. Rights management

The model *(see below)* is drawn from an analysis of the seven areas of this framework, in order to:

- define the tasks involved in implementing each of the key areas;
- identify the key costs associated with these tasks and indicate the factors which will reduce or increase costs;
- indicate those costs which are directly or indirectly related to preservation.

Figure 2. Cost model

Area of framework	Elements to consider		Preservation costs
1. Creation	• Level of control • Overall costs • Best practice costs • Data centre costs	➛	• Promoting best practice • Cleaning up digital resources
2. Selection/ evaluation	• Collection policy • Technical/practical criteria for evaluation • Complexity	➛	• Practical and technical evaluation
3. Data management	• Documentation • Validation (assessment, copying, refreshment) • Data structure conversion • Data storage • 'Data archaeology'	➛	• Reading/editing/ managing documentation • Validation (assessment, copying, refreshment) • Data structure conversion • Off-line archive storage • File recovery from media; crypt-analysis of files of unknown origin
4. Resource disclosure	• Online resource discovery agents • Gateways • Online catalogues	➛	• Post-preservation disclosure costs
5. Data use	• Online access • Digital distribution media	➛	• Post-preservation use costs
6. Data preservation	• Technology preservation		• Keep old hardware/ software • Third party service costs
	• Technology emulation		• Third party service costs
	• Digital information migration	➛	• Change media (recording; archival storage) • Backward compatibility (set up; run; check) • Interoperability (test; set up; run; check) • Convert to standard forms (agree form; test; run; test delete)
7. Data use/rights	• Usage restrictions? • Depositor/user rights	➛	• Clearance, management and authentication costs

5.3 Creation costs

Decisions made when a digital resource is created will have a significant impact on the options subsequently available for its future management, use and preservation. They will also significantly affect the cost of those options. Some organisations involved in preservation are able to exert considerable control over the creation process, while others have little or no influence.

Two organisations which have taken measures to control the life-cycle of the digital record – the Public Record Office (PRO) and the Natural Environment Research Council (NERC) – have already been described. Others are also in a position to influence the creators of digital resources. For example, the Arts and Humanities Data Service (AHDS) serves a specific community, which it has been able to target to explain the benefits of depositing digital resources with AHDS data centres. The Data Archive also specifies technical criteria and preferred data standards which depositors are encouraged to adopt. Increasingly, these centres will also be able to advise scholars and researchers in the humanities on the best practices for creating, documenting and depositing their digital resources.

Many other organisations, on the other hand, have no influence on their depositors. There will continue to be many cases where valuable digital resources will be discovered or deposited which have not been adequately managed or documented. In these cases collection managers will have to make difficult decisions about whether they can afford to take the necessary remedial action. Some of the issues and the techniques involved in 'rescuing' such data are discussed in the next chapter.

One of the biggest problems which data centres all face is in trying to 'clean-up' digital resources. The creators of a digital resource are best equipped to validate and document it. If they fail to do this, then the cost of 'clean-up' at a later stage, when most of the context will have been lost, is conservatively estimated to be ten times greater. In many cases it is impractical to attempt to clean-up digital resources retrospectively, resulting in rejection and loss of the data.

Clearly, the adoption of 'best practice' at the data gathering and creation stage can help simplify the task of managing and preserving the digital resource thereafter. And simplification will result in reduced costs.

Data centres, therefore, cannot ignore the creation stage – even if it is outside their direct control. They face two major cost areas relating to the creation stage.

- The cost of promoting good practice to depositors. This can include posting guidance notes on Web pages, running courses for defined user groups, educating funding bodies, and incorporating guidance notes in funding literature. All data centres should invest at least some resources in this preventative measure.

- The cost of correcting mistakes and examples of bad practice at the creation stage. The less spent on the first area, the more they will have to spend on the second.

On a per digital resource basis, the second costs will far outweigh the first. There is theoretically no limit to the amount of money that data centres could spend on cleaning-up deposited digital resources. There are three practical ways of limiting these costs:

- Where the data centre has a fixed budget, allocate a maximum figure to 'clean-up' activities.
- Define a basic standard. Valuable resources which fall below that standard are brought up to that standard but not taken beyond it.
- Stipulate that digital resources which do not meet a minimum standard in areas such as documentation will be rejected.

Both the promotional (best practice) and the corrective (clean-up) costs relate directly and indirectly to preservation.

5.4 Selection and evaluation (acquisition) costs

The selection of digital resources will be based on the centre's collection policy. The costs associated with evaluating digital resources – assessing them against a series of technical and practical criteria – relate directly to preservation. How easily can the resources be managed, catalogued, accessed by end users and preserved by the data centre?

The level of cost involved will depend on the size and complexity of the digital resource and how well documented it is.

5.5 Data management costs

Data management covers all the tasks involved in managing a digital resource once it has been accepted into a collection.

The ***documentation*** supplied with a digital resource should describe its structure, contents, provenance and history. Centres must check the documentation, edit or add to it, if necessary, make it available to users and keep it up to date. There is a growing need to hold documentation in digital format, so if it is only available on paper there is an extra task involved in digitising it.

Even where the documentation provided is good, reading and studying it incurs a cost. Where it is poor, then clearly the costs increase dramatically as the centre has to test the digital resource and produce additional documentation. Managing the documentation and converting it to digital format can also prove very costly, particularly if the data centre holds a large number of digital resources and there is a significant volume of paper documentation for each resource.

The costs associated with reading, editing and managing the documentation for a digital resource are directly related to preservation. Without documentation it is extremely difficult to ascertain whether a resource can be preserved, or to determine the best strategy for its preservation.

Validation covers a number of procedures, which are together designed to ensure the integrity of the digital resource. They include:

- Assessment, to ensure that the resource is complete as documented, that it is functioning properly and operates on the specified hardware and software environments, and that it is consistent.
- Copying, to provide a back-up in the event of the media being destroyed or damaged.
- Refreshing, to protect against the corruption that would result from any deterioration of the media.

This is an iterative process and so costs are repeated several times during the lifetime of a resource. The costs associated with assessing, copying and refreshing a digital resource all relate directly to preservation.

Data structure covers the way in which a digital resource has been formatted, compressed and encoded, together with any changes which the data centre may decide to make to these. The way in which the resource was originally created will play a large part in determining the level of cost involved in structuring it for future storage and access.

For example, if the resource was created on a proprietary application and deposited in a proprietary format not supported by the data centre, then significant costs would be involved in converting it to a standard format for long term storage and management. These costs clearly relate directly to preservation. However, the costs associated with conversion to a preferred format for delivery to users are outside the preservation remit.

Data storage options are influenced by the resources available, the volume of data to be stored and the way in which they will be used and preserved. In determining costs we should distinguish between online or near-line storage set up to meet the access requirements of users and the management requirements of the centre, and off-line storage set up specifically to meet the preservation requirements of the centre. None of the costs associated with the active management of digital resources relates directly to preservation (although a percentage of the costs, associated with migration, refreshing, etc., would have an indirect relation). The costs associated with the off-line archive storage facility all relate directly to preservation.

'***Data archaeology***' may be required to process incomplete data or analyse files of unknown origin. This is discussed in detail in chapter 6.

5.6 Resource disclosure costs

Resource disclosure concerns the way in which information about a specific digital resource is made available to end users. This information will depend on the resource discovery tools that are implemented for the collection as whole. Examples include resource discovery agents, logically ordered gateways and online catalogues.

While the costs associated with these online resource discovery tools do not in most cases relate to preservation, once the object has moved from active life into an archive there are costs involved in discovering, extracting and preparing the object for use.

5.7 Data use costs

This area covers the costs associated with delivering the digital resources to end users. The costs depend upon the structure of the specific digital resource, how it is stored, and how the user needs to access it – which may involve conversion to different delivery formats. Various delivery mechanisms are possible, including online and publishing on CD-ROM. However, the costs associated with delivering the digital resources to end users are not related to preservation, again except where the delivery is from the digital archive.

5.8 Data preservation costs

Costs will clearly vary, depending on which preservation strategy is adopted.

Apart from copying and refreshing, which have already been dealt with as part of the validation exercise, the technology preservation strategy involves preserving the original application program, operating system software and computer hardware platform that which were all used to create or access the digital resource.

The costs involved to a data centre adopting this strategy would be of two types:

- After moving to a new hardware and software environment, the cost of keeping the old environment running for a short period of time while working on a migration strategy to cover those valuable digital resources that can only be accessed via applications that will only run on the old environment.

- If subsequently the data centre discovered any valuable old digital resources that could only be accessed via applications that would only run on the old environment, they would need to identify a third party still running the old hardware and software and pay them to load the application and the data, and to convert the data into a standard format which they would be able to preserve and migrate to the new environment.

Both types of cost relate directly to preservation.

Technology emulation involves the additional task of designing emulator programs to run on current and future computer platforms and programming them to mimic the behaviour of specific operating system software.

The cost would take the form of a fee to a third party to cover the use of facilities to emulate the required hardware and software environment, so that the centre could run the application and convert the digital resource to a standard format.

Again, this cost relates directly to preservation.

The four techniques within the ***digital information migration*** strategy can also be divided up into a series of tasks, each of which has a cost associated with it.

The costs associated with changing media are threefold:

- Formatting the digital resource and recording it on the new medium – for example, transferring from compact disk recordable (CD-R) to magnetic tape or from video disk to CD. Two copies are needed – one for active use and one for archive.
- Managing the new medium, including indexing, active and archival storage, and the provision of equipment for access.
- Making copies for distribution.

Of these, the recording costs and the archival storage costs relate directly to preservation. However, the costs of storing the active copy of the new medium and the costs of making copies for users are not related to preservation.

The costs associated with backward compatibility would be relatively low in the short to medium term, provided the applications remain backward compatible. If the collection manager decided to upgrade all files created on version X of the application to version X+1 then, provided it was feasible to write a macro that retrieved each file and saved a copy of each file in the new format, this process could be automated. The costs would include the following:

- setting up the macro and running it;
- checking a subset of the resulting files to ensure no corruption has taken place;

- deleting the previous version of the files (if the collection manager opts to do this).

All relate directly to preservation.

The third technique relies on interoperability between rival popular application programs. The more complex the digital resource the more difficult it is to interchange between two application programs without significant loss of data – and the higher the cost incurred.

As with backward compatibility, this process could be automated. The preservation costs include the following:

- testing the interchange on a range of representative documents;
- setting up the program and running it;
- checking a subset of the resulting files to ensure no corruption has occurred;
- deleting the previous version of the files if required.

The fourth and most popular technique is conversion to standard formats. The simpler the digital resource, the easier – and cheaper – it is to select a standard format and effect the conversion. In many cases the process would be identical to that just described for interoperability. After initial tests have been completed, digital images can be converted automatically from one compression algorithm to another and from one file format to another. Most documents created on Windows applications, for example, can be converted to PostScript files or to Adobe's PDF format.

The main costs which relate to preservation would include:

- agreeing on the preferred standard formats;
- testing the conversion for a specific category of resource;
- running the conversion as a batch process;
- testing a sample of converted resources;
- deleting the old versions if required;
- copying the resulting files.

5.9 Rights management costs

Rights management concerns all the processes involved in defining and upholding the rights of depositors and the users of the data centre. These include intellectual property rights and related legal issues such as data protection and confidentiality.

The rights vested in a resource may determine not only how the resource can be accessed and used but also how and whether it can legally be preserved by a third party. The costs associated with rights management can be substantial and may prove to be the highest cost area for the process of digital archiving.

5.10 The cost model in practice

The Cimtech cost model offers a schematic basis for examining digital preservation costs in more detail as those involved in the process explore the options available and the techniques involved. Practical experience will add flesh to the bones, so that in time more sophisticated models will evolve, which managers can begin to use when drawing up budgets and project plans.

The following example applies the model to a real-life organisation involved in the business of data collection and preservation.

The British Oceanographic Data Centre (BODC) was set up in 1989 as NERC's designated data centre for marine data to carry out the following functions:

- provide data management support for UK marine science;
- maintain and develop the UK's national oceanographic database;
- make oceanographic data available to UK academia, industry and government;
- develop innovative marine data products and digital atlases;
- collaborate on behalf of the UK in international exchange and management of oceanographic data.

Creation

Most of the data sets managed by BODC result from major experiments or surveys conducted at sea. Managing oceanographic data involves eight stages:

1. Pre-cruise planning
2. Pre-cruise calibration
3. Data collection at sea and log of activities
4. In situ calibration
5. Data processing, calibration and quality control, at sea and post cruise
6. Production of publishable data set (fully worked up, quality checked, labelled and documented)
7. Data as an end product
8. Application-independent database (available for secondary usage, to create other databases, products, etc.)

While BODC promotes the production of good data as an end in itself, the scientists involved in the experiments rarely have the time or resources to complete steps five and six. Once they have collected the data and carried out selective processing on subsets of interest to them, their first concern is the publication of scientific papers.

The result is that the data deposited with BODC are often incomplete and therefore unusable by others. The centre must spend time and resources processing the data – which would be unnecessary, had all the steps had been completed in the first place. BODC describes this frustrating and expensive task as 'data archaeology'. The centre has tried to stipulate to depositors how data should be processed and documented, but scientists are overstretched and do not have the resources to do it. Often the task is delegated to junior staff and data can be lost.

Recently the centre has taken a different approach, providing a data management service to the cruises. BODC staff accompany the expedition in order to collect, process and document the data as they are created. The cost of providing this service is justified when compared to the overall cost of gathering the data, which often amounts to £10,000 per day. One recent project which has benefited from this approach is OMEX 1. The overall cost of the project was £10 million, while the data management cost £300,000 – approximately 3 per cent of the total budget. Overall, staff have produced 600 data sets on CD-ROM, holding the data gathered on some 47 cruises.

Selection and evaluation

BODC is increasingly involved in the planning stage of new projects and, as just described, in managing the data gathering and management processes. Where the centre is heavily involved in the data creation stage there is less need to carry out selection and evaluation activities as the quality and integrity of the data have already been established before deposit.

Data management

As a general rule, BODC estimates that on a new project some 3-5 per cent of the budget goes on data management.

The centre always aims to publish the data for a project in an application-independent database so that it can be widely used and more easily preserved. Most of the data is alphanumeric, which can be loaded into databases. The centre is now starting to produce electronic documentation using Adobe Acrobat.

However, the data for half of the older experiments or cruises have never been worked up. They are archived, but cannot easily be published, so their value is diminished. This represents a significant data management problem.

It can take BODC five years to work up the data and produce published data sets for a major project. During that time the data sets are managed online using an Oracle relational database engine and made available with password protection to members of the team. All the data are backed up on recordable CDs and digital archive tape (DAT).

Resource disclosure

The bulk of the effort goes into structuring the data for each project, organising the data and providing finding aids for the data sets on CD-ROM. From operating principally as a data archive with some publishing activities, BODC is now primarily a data publisher with a back-up archive function.

Data use

The main method of data distribution is now via published CD-ROMs. A list of all the data sets and an ordering service are provided on the Web. Over the next five years the centre will be producing six CD-ROMs holding data sets gathered on 100 cruises.

Data preservation

The centre has adopted a digital information migration strategy. Staff devote a lot of effort to processing and managing the data, both at the creation stage and on receipt at the centre, to ensure they understand and can migrate them as required.

Part of the processing is designed to make the data application-independent. The data sets are loaded into standard relational tables so they can be imported into spreadsheets and a wide range of relational database engines.

Data sets stored on 4,000 magnetic tapes, built up when the centre started, have now all been transferred to recordable CDs. All new data sets are stored on recordable CDs and tape.

Rights management

The centre follows the policies outlined in the NERC Data Policy Handbook, so contract administration is usually a standardised process.

Overall preservation

In total eighteen BODC staff are engaged in the activities described above.

- six handle promotion of best practice and support to cruises (creation), and selection and rights management;
- eight handle data management and preservation;
- two handle resource disclosure;
- two handle data use.

Overall, six of the eighteen staff (one third) carry out activities which relate directly to preservation.

6 **rescuing** digital materials

6.1 Preservation as rescue

So far this report has discussed the choices available for digital preservation very much in the sense of forward planning – following a set of logical, ordered steps in order to ensure the preservation of digital material. However, this is not always possible. What if one, or more, of these steps has been omitted? Documentation may be missing. Copying, refreshing or routine back-ups may not have been carried out. What if disaster strikes in the form of fire, flood or accident? Or if media have been allowed to deteriorate to the extent that the data they hold are impaired? How can such resources be recovered? In these cases, preservation takes the form of rescue.

Recreating lost data can be very expensive. For example, the US National Security Association has estimated that to recreate only 20 megabytes of data in a US engineering firm would cost $64,400. For some organisations, the loss of data may be catastrophic, resulting in the loss of business and eventually in closure. In certain cases, it may even be impossible to recreate the data.

Data recovery, on the other hand, is the attempt to salvage damaged media and to recapture the digital sequences that make up the information they contain. The demand for data recovery is such that there are now several professional companies specialising in data recovery techniques.

The 'horror stories' recounted below illustrate some of the problems that have arisen. Many organisations will at some point be faced with the challenge of recovering data from difficult (although probably less dramatic) situations. Even the best thought out strategies for digital preservation may have to include some element of data rescue – the 'data archaeology' carried out by BODC, described in the previous chapter, is a good example.

6.2 What can go wrong?

The factors which may contribute to data loss include:

- ***Damage to, or degradation of, the media on which the data are stored.*** Damage may be caused by disaster – fire, flood or accident. After the Challenger Space Shuttle disaster, for example, magnetic tapes holding valuable data were immersed in seawater for six seeks. They were recovered from off the Florida coast still within the instrumentation tape recorders, which were still intact but had broken open as a result of the impact. Three of the six recorders had been corroded by the effects of the seawater and galvanic activity between the magnesium in the tape reels and other metal components, such as the recorder case. The tapes were coated in salt deposits. The magnetic coating had disappeared in some reel segments and the tape substrate was eroded chemically in others. When an attempt was made to unwind the tapes, it was discovered that the recording side had stuck to the back of the tape, making unwinding impossible without destroying the data. Deterioration may also occur as a result of much less spectacular forces – through age, neglect, storage in unsuitable conditions, use in faulty equipment, or careless handling. Though the causes may be more mundane, the effects are similar – valuable information is rendered inaccessible.

- ***Poor management, compounded by missing or weak links in the creation, storage and documentation chain.*** A good example of the problems that can occur comes from the opening of the former East German data archives after German re-unification. The archives had been closed down very suddenly during the political upheaval. Machine-readable data had not been cared for in the same way as paper documents. Many files were no longer accessible and the supporting documentation was incomplete or missing. In the former German Democratic Republic (GDR) electronic data had been processed by mainframes in large centralised data processing centres, controlled by the state. All the tasks were carried out on orders from central government areas. PCs and office systems had not been introduced to government offices until shortly before unification. Specialists from the data centres often left to find new jobs, taking with them knowledge, manuals and documentation. To compound the problems some of the equipment and many of the tapes used for storage were in poor physical condition.

- ***Obsolescence, where the hardware or software required to access the data are no longer available.*** Even a planned transition to new software or hardware can develop into a crisis. An example here is provided by the Premier's Correspondence Unit (PCU) at the Government of Ontario, which went 'paperless' in 1993 using Megadocs software from Digital. It was also decided at this stage that the archival record would be created and supported by the creating office – the PCU – on behalf of the Archives of Ontario. Three years later, Digital announced that it would no longer support Megadocs and recommended Linkworks as a replacement. During preparations for the transition some alarming omissions and problems came to light. There had been no archiving of records, originally planned for optical disks – all records were online. The migration to new software would be extremely expensive. The PCU – the creating office – had no hardware platforms to support the Megadocs records, and Megadocs itself was now obsolete. The Archive faced the complete loss of three years of a key record series documenting a direct link between the governed and the premier.

Sometimes a combination of factors is involved. For example, poor management often goes unnoticed until a crisis brings the problems to light.

6.3 Damage to media

Magnetic media are still the most commonly used media for storing digital information. Although disks offer the most convenient storage medium, tapes remain the most widely used for mass storage. There are two types of magnetic media – hard and soft. To achieve permanent magnetism hard media must be subjected to a significant electro-magnetic field, but as a result they achieve high levels of magnetic remanence and coercivity – qualities which make them especially suited to digital data storage. Soft media need lower applied electro-magnetic fields, but have correspondingly lower remanence and coercivity.

Various materials have been used to make magnetic media over the years and research is still being carried out to refine and improve the process. Most media now consist of a fine layer of ferromagnetic materials suspended in a polymer binder, resting on a non-magnetic substrate.

All the components of magnetic media, including the particles, the binder and the substrate, are susceptible to deterioration. Oxidation and corrosion can reduce the magnetic remanence or coercivity of the particles, resulting in loss of data.

Even new media may lack reliability, and it is not uncommon to encounter new tapes which fail. Only a small number of firms make formulas for coating tapes and even fewer actually undertake the coating activity. The quality of the tape production process is crucial to the creation of reliable media, but very little information about this is available to purchasers. Some disasters have resulted from problems in the production process. BASF, for example, released millions of faulty tapes on to the market and were alerted to the problem by users who had been losing large amounts of data.

Magnetic media can deteriorate as a result of physical and chemical changes in the medium itself. The most significant threat is the breakdown of the binder. Tapes absorb water when stored in humid environments. The process of hydrolysis causes the polymer chains, which make up the binder, to disintegrate, and the binder becomes tacky, creating an adhesive build-up that makes the tape almost impossible to play – an affliction known as 'sticky shed syndrome' in which the magnetic media literally 'sheds' off from the backing substrate. The substrate, too, can deteriorate under humid conditions, causing mistracking, where the read head is unable to locate the data.

Faulty storage and mishandling will also cause deterioration. For example, if the tape is wound too loosely, air pockets will form within the pack, allowing moisture to penetrate and encouraging sticky shed syndrome. Winding too closely allows the edges of the tape to protrude beyond the pack where they will bend and tear. Horizontal storage may lead to 'pack slip', which will put stress on the substrate.

The increasing storage densities of magnetic tape, as well as encouraging its use for mass storage, have exacerbated the problems – there is more data to lose.

Data are stored sequentially on tape, which is transported past the read-write heads in a linear fashion. To access the information on a disk, the heads are moved from the edge of the disk toward and away from the centre along the radius. Hard disks are electro-mechanical devices, consisting of platters coated top and bottom with magnetic oxides. They are vulnerable to 'stiction', a combination of friction and sticking which is similar to sticky shed syndrome. If the silica based disk platters are subjected to high temperatures through excessive use or bad storage, the silica becomes sticky and the disk heads stick to the surface. Other common problems are associated with mechanical or electrical system failures.

The way the data are stored and the type of interface the drive is equipped with will affect the prospects of recovering data. Essential data are held in three areas of the disk – partition tables, the boot block and file allocation tables – all with different functions. For example, the boot record is a short program (in machine code) which issues the instruction to load the operating system into memory. It also contains information about the disk, such as the number of bytes per sector and the number sectors per cluster. Even in newer PCs, which come as 'plug and play', the boot record is stored in the first sector of the first track on a disk containing the active operating system, so that if it is damaged it is still possible to access the data stored after it.

Innovations to enhance access times and increase storage densities may introduce new risks of data loss. For example, the servo pattern, which controls the position of the read-write heads is normally stored on a platter with the data. However, increasing storage by scaling down disks means that the track sizes decrease, the amount of information that the servo has to return increases, and thus the size of storage area for the servo also has to increase. To address this problem IBM has introduced a No-ID format which stores the header or ID information in solid state memory rather than on the disk itself. This improves access times, but also creates a risk of information loss by severing the link between the raw data and the information about its location and meaning.

The difficulties with floppy disks mainly concern the way they are housed – in flexible and easy to damage casings, with media segments which can easily become exposed to the elements. The drive heads are more vulnerable to dust, debris or moisture and thus more susceptible to damage.

Optical media, now widely used for both storage and distribution, have problems of their own. Optical disks consist of a multi-layer sandwich and are reconstructed of polymers and metallics. Metallics are susceptible to corrosion and delamination. Polymers deform and degrade. Either may lead to data loss. Scratching the surface of an optical disk can affect the transmission of the laser beam and cause mistracking. Each type has its own shortcomings.

The least stable are magneto-optical discs. The magnetic layer is metallic and therefore subject to corrosion. They are also susceptible to temperature and humidity changes which can cause the magnetic layer to fracture. The reflective layer of CD-ROM disks is generally made from aluminium that can degrade by oxidation or corrosion. The protective overcoat can deteriorate and expose the aluminium layer to possible damage. The polycarbonate substrate is susceptible to crazing which clouds its definition. Both CD-ROM and CD-R (compact disk recordable) may be damaged by abrasions, dirt and oil residues, temperature and humidity. WORM (write once read many) disks, as with other optical media, are susceptible to changes in the optical properties of the recording layer which result in data loss.

What is the life expectancy of these media? Optical media have a longer life expectancy than magnetic media, and manufacturers make great claims for their durability. How much data loss or how many errors must occur before we can say that a particular tape or disk has reached the end of its useful life? There is no standardised test methodology for predicting life expectancy. And, as we have already seen, so much depends on conditions of storage and handling.

6.4 Recovering damaged media

What techniques are available for restoring data from damaged media? Most data can be rescued, given sufficient time and money-the value of the data must be weighed against the cost of the recovery. Many of the techniques require technical expertise. Here are some examples of what can be done.

- Sticky shed syndrome can be overcome by heat treatment. Heating the tapes for 24-72 hours at 45-55°C can help clear the low molecular weight oils and residues from the tape surface; they are either melted back into the tape or evaporated off. However, this does not reverse the syndrome. Rather, it allows the tapes to be played again in order to copy the data to a more stable medium.
- The only way to tackle mistracking is to re-spool the tape. If the tape is left for a reasonable length of time before re-use, the distorted substrate may be reconditioned.
- While water will damage tapes over time, its effects are not immediately apparent. The absorption rate is slow and tapes can survive in clean water

for days, even weeks. Tapes exposed to contaminants in the water, such as salt or mud, can be rinsed in distilled water or cleaned in soapy water.

- Drying tapes is a delicate operation and is best done naturally at room temperature.
- Disks may be cleaned and dried in the same way as tapes. The disk tracks are laid down as concentric circles, or one continuous spiral, so the disk should not be wiped in a circular motion, but from the inside out.
- Fire damage can be much more severe. If the tapes have suffered extreme temperatures, the substrate and binder may have melted, making it impossible to unwind. However, even here some recovery may be possible using thermal reconditioning processes.

New techniques for data recovery may emerge in the next few years. One example is magnetic force microscopy (MFM) which developed from research into the use of atomic force microscopes. It is possible to examine the surface of a disk or tape using a magnetic force microscope and, in the case of damaged disks, by increasing the sensitivity of the MFM, to observe the data in the damaged area. In other words, it may be possible literally to read the magnetic tracks on the disk and to use optical recognition technologies to recapture the digital sequences.

6.5 Recovering missing links in the creation, storage and documentation chain

Retrieving the raw data is insufficient on its own to recreate the digital resource which is at risk. Archivists also need information about how the data are structured, including compression and encoding, in order to reconstruct and interpret the digital sequences. When data are recovered from old media, or from media of unknown provenance, this information is often incomplete or missing altogether.

When tapes and disks were first developed for computer data storage there was considerable transparency in the layout of the data on the storage device. The 0s and 1s of the binary data being recorded were directly related to the patterns of magnetisation on the storage medium. However, responding to demands for greater storage capacity, manufacturers began to use a variety of techniques to pack more data on the storage medium with the result that stored data have lost the transparency that was evident in earlier systems.

Compression techniques allow more data to be stored, but without the decompression algorithm the raw data cannot be returned to their intended form. Compression techniques usually work separately with each data block, so the patterns in each block may differ considerably. The decoding key should be included as part of the data stream. But if no information is available on the compression method used, it cannot be assumed that decoding one pattern will necessarily work for all the others.

The basic method of recording data on a magnetic surface is known as NRZ (Non Return to Zero). This allows a 1 bit to be represented by a change in magnetic polarity and a 0 bit by no change. However, there are many different ways of encoding data, and in the absence of any documentation to identify the encoding method used, anyone hoping to restore the data will face a daunting task.

Specialist companies use a mixture of specially designed hardware and software to recover data of this kind. Very often, though, the crucial factor is experience, the ability to recognise familiar structures and to piece together the vital information from the scraps of surviving evidence. The process has been compared to deciphering enemy radio messages during the war – work which was carried out with stunning success by Alan Turing at Bletchley Park.

6.6 Overcoming obsolescence

As discussed in chapter 4, migration to new hardware and software platforms generally represents the best strategy for preserving digital information. Computer operating environments change and develop very quickly, making migration both an essential and an ongoing process. Nevertheless, there will always be cases where data collections are found which are only accessible via software and hardware which have already become obsolete. Recovering data from obsolete systems is an area of particular interest to archives, libraries, researchers and academic institutions.

A number of specialist companies provide obsolescence recovery services. Such companies generally maintain a 'library' of peripheral devices and can build or adapt existing platforms to read outdated data, allowing them to be transferred to new software or hardware. These services are not cheap – but they do cost less than recreating the data from scratch.

In some cases the interest and value lie, not so much in the data (or content), but in the appearance and actual workings of hardware and software. Here, the challenge is to find ways of allowing the hardware and software to function in the way originally intended, to 'archive' the nuts and bolts of outdated technology. The techniques include restoration, simulation and emulation.

The Computer Conservation Society, a joint venture between the Science Museum and the British Computer Society, has undertaken work in the restoration of early computers and the recreation of software necessary to run them. The work involves designing and building electronic circuits to read data for which no documentation exists, and developing software to explore the structure of the data captured.

Simulation is the attempt to imitate the functions of a piece of hardware or software. Work on the Ferranti Pegasus, an early computer, has compared the two techniques: the restoration of the original machine to working order, and the construction of a simulation to run in a windows environment on a PC-compatible machine.

Emulation imitates the internal design of hardware platforms and operating system software, allowing the original software to be run. Numerous emulators have been produced for early computer games and console games, and the technique is now also attracting interest from software companies and computer scientists.

While these techniques do not in themselves offer an effective solution to the problems posed by technological change, their efforts are not just of historical value. Experience of building emulators may help to restore valuable data that are otherwise inaccessible, and the expertise gained in restoration projects may help with the 'detective work' that is necessary in piecing together incomplete data.

The faster the pace of technological change, the more urgent is the need to find ways of overcoming obsolescence. Research is continuing to explore new techniques for data recovery. One promising new development is retargetable binary translation (RBT). A binary translator automatically translates a binary executable program from one machine running a particular operating system and using a particular file format, to another platform running a different operating system and using a different file format. It has three parts:

- The front-end works on the source code of the program on the machine which it depends on, disassembling it and converting it to a transitional format.
- The middle-end, which is independent of machine and operating system, performs the core analysis for translation, optimising the code where necessary.
- The final stage, the back-end, generates the code for the second machine, using the binary file formats of the host operating system, and is dependent on that machine. It performs this task using conventional compiler code generation techniques.

A great deal of research is being devoted to this area. The aims is to develop general, platform-independent techniques for binary translation, and to provide tools that will make software available quickly on new machines, without requiring source code or re-programming.

After this glimpse into the future, we should now return to the case histories introduced at the beginning of this section. What did they do? How did they recover their data?

6.7 Recovering the Challenger data tapes

The National Aeronautics and Space Administration (NASA) asked IBM to assist in recovering the data. They wanted to understand the mechanisms of the interlayer adhesion, to develop a process to clean and unwind the tapes, and to transfer the data on to new tapes so that NASA could piece together the reasons why the shuttle had so disastrously crashed. In the process they also wanted to find ways of avoiding this type of problem in future. The recovery team started by analysing a tape identical to that used in the shuttle in order to identify the chemical processes involved in the interlayer adhesion. They also examined the condition of the tape binder to establish whether any special handling would be necessary because of its physical deterioration. They studied three of the shuttle's recorders and the tapes they held, which contained information on engine operations, the voice recordings and the conditions of two satellites in the cargo bay.

Various processes were used to analyse the tape samples: scanning electron microscope (SEM) with energy dispersive analysis of X-rays (EDAX); X-ray fluorescence; diffraction; and chemical analysis. These techniques revealed white deposits on the edges as well as in isolated areas of the recording side; they were also found on the back side of the tape from the transferred recording side. Further analysis identified the deposits on the recording side as magnesium hydroxide. An experiment was conducted to confirm that the magnesium hydroxide was responsible for the interlayer adhesion, rather than the urethane rich binder degradation found on the back side of the tapes. Dilute aqueous acid, which dissolves magnesium hydroxide, was found to be effective in releasing the adhesion.

Having identified the chemical events which had caused the interlayer adhesion, the team had to find a method of applying the solution which would allow the fragile tapes to be unwound without further damage. They removed the eroded hub from the tapes and mounted them on a spring-loaded plastic ring. The tapes were then soaked in a tank containing a solution of aqueous acid, followed by a series of methanol washes and water rinses, and finally relubricated. After chemical treatment the tapes were unwound very carefully at a speed of 0.15m per minute.

The team realised that the tapes were very fragile and would only stand one playing to retrieve the data. They re-recorded the data in analogue mode to reduce the difficulties with signal amplification. NASA was able to read more than 90 per cent of the data from one recorder and 100 per cent from the others – allowing us, the public, to hear the voices of the astronauts immediately prior to the explosion.

The recovery team recommended that NASA no longer use magnesium as the hub material to avoid the problems of interlayer adhesion in future.

6.8 Recovering electronic records after German re-unification

Of particular interest to archivists was the Kaderdatenspeicher, or database of party functionaries, which contained personal data on 331,980 staff members of East German government agencies. At least one copy of the database is believed to have been destroyed before unification in order to protect party members. The one surviving copy was acquired by the Federal Archives.

As well as the raw data, archivists need the documentation that accompanies the digital material, in order to interpret the data correctly and place them in the relevant context. Where this documentation is missing or incomplete, as in the case of the Kaderdatenspeicher, much detective work is necessary to piece together and decipher the meaning of the data.

The volume labels, headers and first blocks of data were printed out. The volume labels and headers followed IBM format and were therefore easy to read. These data provided details of the content of each tape and an idea of the different applications of the database. At this stage a typical problem emerged: three different ways of expressing dates were found in the volume labels and headers. Many more were found in the data themselves. These included: the fairly standard dd/mm/yy; the day, month, year and decade expressed as a series of characters (e.g. V18); and bit counting, where a bit is counted for every day from a fixed date – very difficult to decipher. Similarly, different methods were used to encode the personal identification number, which every GDR citizen had. It became apparent that without further documentation on the precise structure of the files, it would be extremely difficult to decipher the exact meaning of the data.

The documentation was reconstructed piece by piece from various sources. References to the Kaderdatenspeicher were found in the paper files of the Council of Ministers which had been transferred to the Federal Archives after unification, and these records supplied the information required to decipher the data file structures and codebooks. The East German data processing centres had exchanged information using shared codebooks, and these were used to help identify codes in different data fields. It was also discovered that the data from the Kaderdatenspeicher were closely linked to other government data files, such as the database for Public Education. While these reconstructions helped archivists understand the data file structure, they still had difficulties in interpreting the data. In some cases specialist software was developed to help in this; in others they had to resort to human contact – calling in former employees for assistance. The database is now archived and copies are available for research.

This is a vivid illustration of the need for relevant documentation to support digital material. While it is possible to restore data with incomplete documentation, this is a painstaking, time-consuming – and expensive – exercise.

6.9 Rescuing the records of the Archives of Ontario

The problems faced by the Archives of Ontario were not in the same league as those in the aftermath of a disaster such as a fire or flood. Nevertheless, decisions had to be made quickly in an atmosphere of some stress and urgency, and, perhaps inevitably in such a situation, resulted in a compromise. The Archives, which had no electronic records programme and no emergency resources, was unable to undertake the preservation or migration of the records itself; nor could it take unilateral action to rescue the records.

In the event the Premier's Correspondence Unit arranged the financial and staff resources to migrate those records which dated from an important transition in political power (in 1995), which it felt were necessary for current needs – about 80,000 files. A small selection of records which predated the 1995 political transition – about 22,750 files – were printed out on paper with accompanying printouts of indexes. This was an emergency measure, taken because the resources to migrate to new software were not available, but imperfectly executed as the system was not designed for such an event. Although the records were rescued, in the sense that the data were not irretrievably lost, the opportunity for a planned, orderly transition was missed. Decisions were taken in a hurry and expediency became the priority.

The episode did serve to highlight weaknesses in the system that could be avoided in the future, and the digital stable was finally locked (even though the data had bolted). Schedules have been drawn up for archiving new records on computer-output microfilm (COM).

7 **completing** the jigsaw: managing the digital preservation process

7.1 Drawing the strands together

This report has attempted to outline the key issues in digital preservation and has examined in detail some of the processes involved and the interplay between them:

- The interaction of the stakeholders: their attitudes to digital preservation; the rights they expect to be upheld; the responsibilities expected of them and which they are prepared to fulfil.
- The life-cycle of the digital resource and the ways in which different stakeholders' interests influence stages of this life-cycle.
- The techniques for digital preservation, and the technological choices available.
- Tools for evaluating digital resources and selecting appropriate strategies for their long-term preservation.
- Identifying and estimating the costs of preservation.
- Ways in which digital resources may be lost or put at risk through neglect or damage. Methods of rescuing such resources.

Individual organisations will be able to pick out those issues and parts of the process that are of most relevance to their own interests and aims. Each is responsible for a different piece of the jigsaw. However, to achieve the ultimate goal – the long-term preservation of the cultural and intellectual heritage in digital form – we must recognise the interdependence between all the different stages in the creation, use and preservation of digital resources so that we can see the complete picture.

7.2 Managing a digital archive

Figure 3 represents a model for managing an archive facility. The central six functions, stretching from capture through to access and retrieval, are the core of the activity. The overall planning, reporting and administration are essential functions required to run the archive facility.

How the archive is managed and run operationally will have an effect on the whole preservation process. Efficient procedures during archive will reduce

Figure 3: Managing a digital archive

Strategy, policy and planning Security • Configuration planning • Technology watch • IS capacity planning				
Reporting Resource usage • Security exposures • Efficiency and productivity (cost management) • Virus detection • Variance analyses				
Project management Quality control • Security • Resource control • Schedule control • Data transfer control • Workflow control				
Capture Candidate material assessment • Advice • Guidance • Supplier liaison and negotiation	**Preservation engineering** Pre-loading tests • Encapsulation • Testing • QA of builds	**Storage management** Back up/recovery • QA • Testing • Media transfers • Refresh cycles	**Environment engineering** Network • O/S • Cabling • Configuration • Software upgrades	**Access/retrieval** Requirements analysis • Help desk • Virus incident alert • Testing
Administration management Audit • Security marking • Virus checking • HR management • Skill development • Training • Finance • Software licensing • Documentation • Legal services • Procurement • Maintenance contract				

costs not only during capture, but also further back up the business chain of activities, possibly improving the efficiency of the creators themselves. Keeping up with and adapting to the changing technological environment will also influence costs and methods of retrieval and access.

The keys to the success of the archive are confidence and commitment. Increasing confidence in the security of the archive and the integrity of the items is essential to securing the commitment of stakeholders to it.

7.3 Managing The Digital Archive – constructing a 'value chain'

This, in microcosm, is the essence of good practice in digital preservation. We can apply all the principles and procedures of managing a digital archive to the much larger picture of managing digital preservation as a whole.

Here, too, the key concepts are confidence and commitment. For the process to operate in an efficient and cost-effective way requires the commitment and cooperation of all the organisations and groups involved. By managing the complete process as a 'value chain', from capture to retrieval, improvements can be made in the way stakeholders communicate and work together, controlling costs, improving service levels, and raising quality levels.

7.4 A checklist for best practice

In order to achieve this 'value chain', organisations with an interest in digital preservation must complete their part of the jigsaw in as efficient a manner as possible. The following recommendations, proposed by AHDS, outline best practices to be adopted to ensure that data resources suit the purposes for

which they are intended, and their content, appearance, and functionality may be cost effectively preserved over the longer term. They are not all directly relevant to all groups, but they are all essential to building the larger Digital Archive.

Data and collection design

- Whether data resources are being created, accessioned physically into a collection, or made accessible to a defined user community, rigorous evaluation is essential to ensure that the resources serve the purpose for which they are intended at an affordable cost. Data creators, digital collection developers and data archivists should take note of best practice in the evaluation of potential data resources. That evaluation will, at a minimum, entail examination of the resources':
    - contents, scope and relevance to a defined user community or purpose;
    - technical characteristics (structure) and how these influence the resources' fitness for use and long-term maintenance;
    - documentation (whether this is sufficient for the intended use and long-term maintenance);
    - legal terms and conditions which attach to their management and use.
- Such an examination will take place in light of the evaluating organisation's mission, and the funding and technologies which are available to it.

Data creation

- The way in which a data resource may be used, at what cost, and even whether it may be preserved, are influenced principally by decisions taken when creating or including that resource in a collection. Data creators need to be aware of this influence and accordingly of their role in determining the direction of a data resource's future life course.
- Data creators who are interested in ensuring the secondary use and preservation of their resources will adopt standards and best practices. While these reduce the cost involved in securing a data resource's long-term viability and subsequent use, they are not essential to it. Provided that sufficient documentation exists, even data resources produced in idiosyncratic proprietary formats may, with sufficient investment, be emulated or rendered into platform-independent (and thus migratable) formats.
- Data creators should consider the following categories of standards:
    - those which ensure that data can be migrated with minimum content loss across platforms (standard file formats, and compression and encoding techniques);
    - those which ensure that data can be migrated meaningfully between ind-

dividuals and organisations (documentation standards, as devised by specialist communities and curatorial professions);
- those which ensure that data resources are comparable with other like resources (data value standards, as derived by specialist communities);
- those which ensure that data resources suit the purposes for which they are created (as derived by specialist communities).

Data storage and data structures

- These should be chosen to support intended use and/or preservation scenarios.
- In some instances, it may be appropriate to represent and store a data resource in different structures. Academic data archives, for example, may store data in the form in which they were deposited, in a form conducive to their long-term management, and in a number of forms appropriate to their intended uses. Digitisers might similarly store data resources in differently structured versions, for example as high-quality master copies from which other lower-quality distribution copies may be generated, as appropriate, to different users.
- Many stakeholders will need to confront or implement remote data management strategies. These provide particular challenges, for example where remotely managed resources are to be integrated from a user's point of view with data and other information resources stored on site. Successful remote management typically entails agreement with third-party data managers about minimum level data selection, documentation, management, and delivery standards and practices.

Data documentation

- Data documentation is essential to the exchange of data resources between platforms and individuals. At a minimum, it should provide information about a resource's provenance, contents and structure, and about the terms and conditions attached to its subsequent management and use. It should be sufficiently detailed to support:
    - resource discovery (i.e. the location of a resource which is at least briefly described along with many other resources);
    - resource evaluation (i.e. the process by which users determine whether they require access to that resource);
    - resource ordering (i.e. the information which instructs a user about the terms and conditions attached to a resource and how to gain access to it);
    - resource use (i.e. the information which a user may need in order to access the resource's information content);
    - resource management (i.e. administrative information essential to a resource's management as part of a broader collection and including information about location, version control, etc.).

- Where data resources are included or intended for inclusion within broader collections, minimum documentation should be supplied for all resources according to an appropriate standard or standards selected by the collection managers in light of their collection development aims, the kinds of data contained within their collection, and the information requirements of the collection's intended users. Collection managers need to take note of standard documentation practices.

- Those responsible for managing digital collections are usually best able to determine how data resources in that collection should be documented, while those responsible for creating resources within a collection are usually best able to supply information required for its adequate documentation. The documentation of data which is included in collections should result from a dialogue between data creators and data managers.

Preservation strategies

- **Data migration is the preferred preservation strategy for data resources which are created with platform-independent data standards or which can be migrated into such data standards with minimal content loss. Such resources may be preserved by ensuring their readability on contemporary media and, where necessary, by reformatting them as required by ascendant standard regimes.**

- Migration is not appropriate for the following kinds of resources. For these, technical preservation (except in the case of the second) or emulation may be preferred.

    - those in which the hardware platform makes an essential contribution to the resource's meaning and/or to the experience of its use (e.g. video games, game boys);
    - those where data are stored in undocumented proprietary formats (i.e. proprietary information systems which store data in binary formats);
    - those where data are stored in undocumented formats and bundled with access software which is also undocumented (e.g. commercial CD-ROM products)

Preservation practices (with regard exclusively to data migration)

- **Data preservation entails the creation and maintenance of archive copies of data files. Archive copies of a data resource are independent of any online representation and as such are distinguished from back-up copies of the same resource. Periodic and systematic back-up of online data resources is not in itself a sufficient preservation strategy.**

- Archive copies should be stored on industry standard digital tape or on other approved contemporary media as may arise.

- Archive copies should be available on- and off site. Off-site copies should be stored at a safe distance from on-site copies to ensure they are unaffected by any natural or man-made disaster affecting the latter.
- Archive copies should be written with different software to protect data against corruption from malfunctioning or virus- or bug-ridden software.
- Archive copies should be made to comparable magnetic media purchased from different suppliers to guard against faults introduced by the media's suppliers into their products or into batches of their products.
- Data files stored as archive copies should be migrated to new media. Migration should take place within the minimum time specified by the media's suppliers for the media's viability under prevailing climatic conditions. In addition, media should be checked periodically for their readability. Such checking may be conducted automatically by archive systems according to parameters set by system operators.
- The integrity of data files should be checked periodically using checksum and similar procedures. Such procedures may be implemented automatically by the archive system according to parameters set by system operators
- Proper preservation is expensive, requiring substantial computing infrastructure and expertise not normally accessible to all those involved in the development and management of data collections, even as data archives. Those individuals and organisations which lack the appropriate facilities should conduct a cost benefit analysis to determine whether the data preservation functions they require may be most cost effectively outsourced to a specialist computing service, data bank , or other organisation.

Data use

- **Data creators' fear that their data may be put to unwarranted or inappropriate uses is a principal deterrent to the development of high-quality data collections. Robust and enforceable user agreements, combined with user registration, authentication, and other security measures, will go some way toward alleviating this fear and enhancing collection development activities. Investigation into the development and widespread deployment of such mechanisms is a priority.**
- Users and data developers alike show a growing preference for making data resources available over the Internet via World Wide Web browsers. Web delivery is an appropriate and cost effective means of delivering some resources. For others, it adds a significant development cost and may reduce a resource's functionality.

8 **key** recommendations and follow-up activities

8.1 Recommendations

1. ***Raise awareness*** about the importance and value of digital preservation, and about the roles played by various stakeholders in the preservation process. The effort must be targeted appropriately for different stakeholders and be sensitive to the role that those stakeholders play in preservation. Stakeholders include:

    - universities, funding and other agencies, which invest in the development of digital resources and which need to develop data preservation policies;
    - individual and organisational 'data creators' in the heritage, library, archive, and scholarly communities;
    - organisations and centres, which routinely manage digital collections (data archives and data banks, but equally universities, libraries and heritage organisations);
    - the software industry, which may supply tools capable of automating some processes essential to the production of preservable data resources.

2. ***Encourage communication*** between and collaboration among the various sectors currently involved in relevant research and development work, including scholarly, library, heritage and data archiving (both public and commercial) communities.

3. ***Develop guidelines*** pertaining to standards and best practices which promise to increase the likelihood for, and reduce the cost of, digital preservation. Such guidelines should be prepared for different classes of digital resources (which need to be defined) and for the different purposes to which any one class may be put.

4. ***Investigate strategies*** for organising and funding a preservation centre or network of preservation centres for scholarly, library, and heritage data whose long-term preservation is not otherwise secured.

5. ***Develop criteria*** for *bona fide* or approved data archives and a list of organisations which meet those criteria.

6. ***Develop a checklist*** which may be used to determine the complexity and cost of preserving different classes of digital resources. This approach should be developed with reference to a cross-section of archiving organisations, as appropriate, to ensure the best possible coverage of all digital resource classes.

7. ***Conduct further research*** into the feasibility and cost of technology preservation, technology emulation, and preservation of 'dynamic' data resources. Research topics pertaining to emulation include:

    - the viability of the preservation of media access devices;
    - the use of magnetic force microscopy to recover data from magnetic media;
    - the use of cryptography to decode bit sequences.

    In addition, effort should be directed towards:

    - developing data-loss case histories;
    - systematically collecting hardware and software documentation, including designs;
    - developing a media quality index taking account of factors such as adhesion, abrasivity, durability, chemical stability and error rates, and marking every piece of storage media with a quality rating.

8. Actions which pertain expressly to the *preservation of electronic publications*:

    - develop a definition of an 'electronic publication';
    - establish a joint coordinating body to determine the allocation of electronic publications between legal deposit libraries;
    - raise awareness amongst public bodies that records created by them are subject to the Public Records Act.

8.2 The CEDARS Project

Some of the issues raised in this report are now being addressed by the CEDARS Project, which is being directed by the Consortium of University Research Libraries (CURL) under the Electronic Libraries (eLib) Programme.

Academic libraries have a new and complex responsibility for ensuring that digital resources remain accessible to users over the long term, irrespective of whether the burden for physically preserving those resources falls to the library or to a third party agency. The need to devise strategies for digital preservation is pressing; such strategies will need to encompass all forms of digital information resources. The CEDARS Project therefore aims to address strategic, methodological and practical issues, and to provide guidance for libraries in best practice for digital preservation. The Project will produce:

- guidelines for developing collection management policies which will ensure the long-term viability of any digital resources included in the collection;
- demonstrator projects to test and promote the technical and organisational feasibility of a chosen strategy for digital preservation;
- methodological guidelines developed by the demonstrator projects providing

guidance about how to preserve different classes of digital resources;
- clearly articulated preferences about data formats, content models and compression techniques which are more readily and cost-effectively preserved;
- publications of benefit to the whole higher education community, available on the World Wide Web.

appendix 1

Studies on the preservation of electronic materials commissioned by the Digital Archiving Working Group

Beagrie, N. and Greenstein, D. (1998): ***A strategic policy framework for creating and preserving digital collections***. British Library Research and Innovation Report 107. London: The British Library.

Bennett, J.C. (1997) ***A framework of data types and formats, and issues affecting the long term preservation of digital material***. British Library Research and Innovation Report 50. London: The British Library.

The Data Archive, University of Essex (1998) ***An investigation into the digital preservation needs of universities and research funders: the future of unpublished research materials***. British Library Research and Innovation Report 109. London: The British Library.

Haynes, D., Streatfield, D., Jowett, T., and Blake, M. (1997) ***Responsibility for digital archiving and long term access to digital data***. British Library Research and Innovation Report 67. London: The British Library.

Hendley, T. (1998) ***Comparison of methods and costs of digital preservation***. British Library Research and Innovation Report 106. London: The British Library.

Matthews, G., Poulter, A., and Blagg, E. (1997) ***Preservation of digital materials policy and strategy issues for the UK: report of a meeting on the CPA/RLG report, December 1996***. British Library Research and Innovation Report 41. London: The British Library.

Ross, S. and Gow, A. (1999) ***Digital Archaeology: The Recovery of Digital Materials at Risk***. British Library Research and Innovation Report 108. London: The British Library.

appendix 2

References and bibliography

Bhushan, B. and Phelan, R.M. (1987) Overview of Challenger Space-Shuttle tape-data recovery study, ***IEEE Transactions on Magnetics***, 23(5), 3179-83.

The British Library (1996) ***Proposal for the legal deposit of non-print publications to the Department of National Heritage from the British Library***. London: The British Library Board.

The Data Archive, University of Essex ***Guide to depositing data***. The Acquistion Section, The Data Archive, University of Essex, Wivenhoe Park, Colchester, Essex, CO4 3SQ (http://hds.essex.ac.uk/).

Department of National Heritage (1997) ***Legal deposit of publications: a consultation paper***. London: Department of National Heritage.

Fresko, M. (1996) ***Long term preservation of electronic materials***. Report of a JISC/British Library Workshop as part of the Electronic Libraries Programme (eLib), organised by UKOLN, 27-28 November 1995, University of Warwick. British Library R&D Report 6328. London: The British Library.

Hedstrom, M. ***Digital preservation: a time bomb for digital libraries*** (http:/www.uky.edu/~kiernan/DL/hedstrom.html).

Library and Information Commission (1997) ***New library: the people's network***. London: Library and Information Commission Working Group on Information Technology.

Lowry, R.K. (1998) ***Data management for the OMEX I project: a case study***. British Oceanographic Data Centre, Proudman Oceanographic Laboratory, Bidston Observatory, Birkenhead, Merseyside L43 7RA.

National Library of Australia, National Preservation Office (1997) ***Statement of principles: preservation of and long-term access to Australian digital objects*** (http://www.nla.gov.au/3/npo/natco/princ.html).

Natural Environment Research Council (1998) ***Formal NERC data policy statement***, version 2.0, February 1998. Swindon: NERC.

Public Record Office (1998) ***Final guidelines on the management of electronic records from office systems*** (http://www.pro.gov.uk/eros/guidelinesfinal.pdf).

Waters, D. and Garrett, J. (1996) ***Preserving digital information***. Report of the Task Force on Archiving of Digital Information commissioned by the Commission on Preservation and Access and the Research Libraries Group. Washington, D.C.: Commission on Preservation and Access. (http://www.rlg.org/ArchTF/)

Wettengel, M. (1998) German unification and electronic records, the example of the Kaderdatenspeicher. ***In History and electronic artefacts***, edited by E. Higgs. Oxford.

appendix 3

Acronyms

AHDS	Arts and Humanities Data Service
ASCII	American Standard Code for Information Interchange
BFI	British Film Institute
BODC	British Oceanographic Data Centre
CAD	Computer Aided Design
CBT	Computer Based Teaching
CD-ROM	Compact Disk Read-Only Memory
CEDARS	CURL Exemplars in Digital ARchiveS project
CER	Center for Electronic Records
COM	Computer-Output Microfilm
CPA	Commission on Preservation and Access
CURL	Consortium of University Research Libraries
DAT	Digital Archive Tape
ECMS	Electronic Copyright Management System
EDAX	Energy Dispersive Analysis of X-rays
eLib	Electronic Libraries Programme
ESRC	Economic and Social Research Council
ftp	file transfer protocol
GDR	German Democratic Republic
GIS	Geographical Information System
HEI	Higher Education Institution
HEFC	Higher Education Funding Council
HTML	HyperText Markup Language
IBM	International Business Machines
IGES	Initial Graphics Exchange Specification
IS	Information Systems
IT	Information Technology
JISC	Joint Information Services Committee of the Higher Education Funding Councils
MFM	Magnetic Force Microscopy
MIDI	Musical Instrument Digital Interface
MPEG	Motion Picture Experts Group
NARA	National Archives and Records Administration

NASA	National Aeronautics and Space Administration
NERC	Natural Environment Research Council
NPO	National Preservation Office
NRZ	Non Return to Zero
O/S	Operating System
OTA	Oxford Text Archive
OUCS	Oxford University Computing Service
PC	Personal Computer
PCU	Premier's Correspondence Unit, Government of Ontario
PDF	Portable Document Format
PRO	Public Record Office
QA	Quality Assurance
RBT	Retargetable Binary Translation
RLG	Research Libraries Group
RTF	Rich Text Format
SCRAN	Scottish Cultural Resources Access Network
SDC	Space Data Centre, Rutherford Appleton Laboratory
SEM	Scanning Electron Microscope
SGML	Standard Generalised Markup Language
TEI	Text Encoding Initiative
TIFF	Tagged Image File Format
ULCC	University of London Computing Centre
V&A	Victoria and Albert Museum
WORM	Write Once Read Many

appendix 4

Members of the Digital Archiving Working Group

Mr Michael Alexander
Manager
Document and Image Processing Systems
British Library

Mr Paul Ayris
Librarian
University College London

Mr Richard Blake
Public Record Office

Ms Nancy Elkington
Member Services Officer
Research Libraries Group

Mr Peter Fox
Librarian
Cambridge University Library

Dr Dan Greenstein
Director
Arts and Humanities Data Service
King's College London

Stephanie Kenna
British Library

Dr Vanessa Marshall
Director
National Preservation Office
British Library

Mr Keith Nettle
Publishing Consultant

Dr Seamus Ross
HATII
University of Glasgow

Mr Chris Rusbridge
Programme Director
Electronic Libraries Programme
University of Warwick

Mrs Alison Walker
Deputy Director
National Preservation Office
British Library

Mrs Bridget Winstanley
The Data Archive
University of Essex